AND HE DWELT AMONG US

A.W. TOZER

Compiled and Edited by James L. Snyder

AND
HE DWELT AMONG US

TEACHINGS FROM THE GOSPEL OF JOHN

Regal

From Gospel Light
Ventura, California, U.S.A.

Published by Regal
From Gospel Light
Ventura, California, U.S.A.
www.regalbooks.com
Printed in the U.S.A.

Library of Congress Cataloging-in-Publication Data
Tozer, A. W. (Aiden Wilson), 1897-1963.
And He dwelt among us / A.W. Tozer ; compiled and edited by James L. Snyder.
p. cm.
ISBN 978-0-8307-4691-0 (trade paper)
1. Bible. N.T. John—Sermons. 2. Christian and Missionary Alliance—Sermons.
3. Sermons, American—20th century. I. Snyder, James L. II. Title.
BS2615.54.T69 2009
252'.099—dc22
2009010047

1 2 3 4 5 6 7 8 9 10 / 15 14 13 12 11 10 09

Rights for publishing this book outside the U.S.A. or in non-English languages are
administered by Gospel Light Worldwide, an international not-for-profit ministry.
For additional information, please visit www.glww.org, email info@glww.org, or write
to Gospel Light Worldwide, 1957 Eastman Avenue, Ventura, CA 93003, U.S.A.

CONTENTS

A PASSION FOR THE LOST

Those familiar with A. W. Tozer usually regard him as the voice of a prophet. He was that for many years, and through his writings, he still is a prophetic voice to the Church of Jesus Christ. However, in *And He Dwelt Among Us,* we hear a slightly different voice from Tozer. Here he ministers not as a prophet but as a pastor with a passion to reach those who are lost.

For more than a year, Dr. Tozer preached weekly on the Gospel of John, one of his favorite books of the Bible. Although he never laid out the entire series of sermons, week by week the Gospel took possession of his mind and soul. One week, a phrase or even a word would capture his heart, and he would lift his congregation to the heights of Spirit-anointed preaching. The Gospel captured his imagination, and he could not turn away from it.

More people acknowledged new life in Christ during this series of sermons than any series Tozer ever preached in Chicago. Always, no matter where he started, he was the shepherd searching for the lost sheep. Oftentimes after the sermon concluded, the congregation would sit in silence because of the intensity of the truth he had expounded. After one such sermon, a longtime member of the congregation confided, "He out Davided David," meaning, of course, that like David, Tozer had a way of presenting truth in a musical frame that set the heart to singing.

Such an effort was daunting even to Tozer. In fact, the series was so elevated in spiritual flavor that it stretched his own preaching ability. "It is going to be a pleasure to expound on this book," he told his congregation, "but a sense of inadequacy has come over me so stunning that I am not able now to call it a pleasure. The impossibility of a man like me saying anything worthwhile about the writings of a man like John has me, quite literally after all these years, paralyzed. But perhaps this will be God's way of reducing the flesh to a minimum and giving the Holy Spirit the best possible opportunity to do His eternal work."

Many congregations would not have the patience to stick with a series such as this for over a year, but in these sermons we see Tozer at his best. There is a temperament in the apostle John that definitely resonated within his own heart, and in this series of teachings we see him reflecting that temperament. While he had no problem challenging Christians on their faith or pointing out the heresies infesting the true Church, in this book he is not simply defending sound doctrine but rather rising to doctrine's high and lofty conclusion.

To Tozer, any doctrine that did not rise to the height of identification with the Lord Jesus Christ was either misunderstood or not properly rooted in Scripture. He believed that there were two sides to doctrine. First, doctrine establishes truth and helps us to recognize developing heresies within the Church and how to deal with them. Second, doctrine is a path to the intimate knowledge of God. All things must point to Him who dwelt among us. Based on a foundation of sound doctrine, the apostle John rises into the rarefied atmosphere of adoration, and Dr. Tozer follows closely in his train.

The Mysticism of John

Tozer believed that John represented the best of the "mystical" thinkers. Of course, describing John in this manner introduces a term that is grossly misunderstood by many today. Tozer realized this fact, but he often said that he would never allow somebody to rob him of anything simply because he or she misused it. He was not afraid to identify with the great host of Christian mystics, going all the way back to the apostle John. And Tozer knew them all.

Although Tozer greatly admired the theology of the apostle Paul, he had a great affinity for the mystical bent of John the apostle. "In the mind of John," he said, "God found a harp that wanted to sit in the window and catch the wind. He found that John had a bird-like sense about him that wanted to take flight all the time. God allowed John, starting from the same premise as the theologian Paul, to mount and soar and sing."

To Tozer, John was like the lark that rose at the break of day, shook the dew of night from its wings and soared to heaven's gate in song. It was not that John soared any higher than Paul, just that he sang a bit sweeter. Paul, the theologian, laid the foundation. Once his foundation had been laid, John got up on the parapet, flapped his wings and took off.

This, perhaps, is why Tozer felt it was so difficult to preach on the Gospel of John. Without a clear, solid doctrinal foundation, it was too easy to go off on some emotional tangent. Tozer was a mystic with his feet on solid doctrinal ground. Without that foundation, he would have been susceptible to making silly and erroneous conclusions. And Tozer did not want to fall into that trap.

With the doctrinal emphasis of the apostle Paul, one could become quite legalistic and cold spiritually. And with the mystical emphasis of the apostle John, one could become so heavenly minded that he was of no earthly good. The combination of these two provided the kind of spiritual experience that was healthy for maturing Christians. Tozer was careful to balance the two.

The Curse of Spiritual Boredom

A great concern of Dr. Tozer's, which he addresses in this book, was in this area of what he called "spiritual boredom." Simply put, this occurs when Christians become addicted to the activity of the world around them to the exclusion of helpful spiritual disciplines. Tozer was concerned that many Christians were more interested in the world around them than the Eternal Word within them.

According to Tozer, spiritual boredom is the consequence of immaturity. The immature are easily bored with anything that is routine. They want to liven up their life with excitement, action and activity, whereas the Christian life should be nurtured by daily disciplines. And, of course, there is the danger that some people do the same thing over and over again and find themselves in some kind of spiritual rut. To maintain a balance in the Christian life is the great secret of maturity.

Tozer believed that this boredom brought certain consequences to the evangelical church in America. "To a large degree, familiarity has brought boredom to the evangelical church, especially in America," he once said. "We have heard the same thing repeated until we are bored. I do not blame those who repeat, because it is necessary that we continue to say the same things. What I complain about is that we are unconscious of that Presence of the one who can take the familiar word and make it brilliantly new. We are dying by degrees in evangelical circles because we are resting in the truth of the Word and are forgetting that there is a Spirit of the Word without which the truth of the Word means nothing to the human spirit at last."

As always, Dr. Tozer offered a solution to counter this spiritual boredom. On one occasion, he offered this spiritual counsel to a young man just starting in the ministry: "Search your soul, do something for yourself, start over, take a day off, get before God, pray through, get something new on you so that you won't be petered out and become one more old beat up preacher who can talk about holy things like it is shop talk . . . who can talk about the name of Jesus Christ without any break in the voice . . . who can talk about heaven without any excitement . . . who can talk about God without any reference."

As you read this book and explore the Gospel of John, allow Tozer's words to cultivate the mystical side of your Christian experience and cure any tendencies you might have toward spiritual boredom.

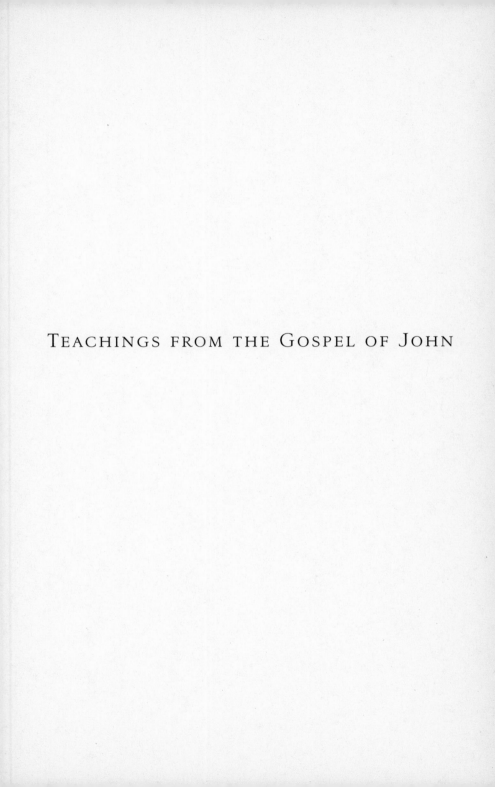

TEACHINGS FROM THE GOSPEL OF JOHN

1

God Has Put Everlasting into Our Souls

In the beginning was the Word, and the Word was with God,
and the Word was God.

John 1:1

Of all the books of the Bible, none presents Christ as supremely as the Gospel of John. I believe the reason it captures our heart and mind so is because of John's approach. Whereas the apostle Paul presents Christ in a theological setting, John uses the mystical setting. In doing so, John does not disregard theology, for there is plenty of theology in his Gospel; rather, he uses theology as a ladder to climb to the heights of Christ's nature.

Some may recoil at my use of the word "mystical," but I believe it accurately describes the personality and temperament of the apostle John. "Mystical," as employed in the Gospel of John and in this book, simply refers to the cultivation of a deep appreciation of the unique nature of Christ and our fascination with Him. From the first verse of the first chapter of John's

Gospel—"In the beginning was the Word, and the Word was with God, and the Word was God"—we are elevated into the realm of "everlasting."

"In the beginning was the Word" (John 1:1). Let us leave that phrase here in the New Testament and, in order to understand it better, go back to the Old Testament. It is characteristic of the wisdom books of the Old Testament that sometimes they contain short passages that get lost in the sand and dust of the ages but are so profound and solid that they are literally building blocks of spiritual thought. Ecclesiastes 3:11 is such a thought: "He hath made every thing beautiful in his time: also he hath set the world in their heart, so that no man can find out the work that God maketh from the beginning to the end."

You might be tempted to pass up this passage and go to a psalm for a little help. But if you will know what the Holy Ghost meant here when He said that God hath set the world in the heart of man, you will not go beyond it. I suspect that buried here under the shifting sands of the desert is a palace with many rooms and much beauty. Let us walk around the palaces, behold the goodly bulwarks thereof and see what we can find.

Psalm 90:2 will give us a light on what Ecclesiastes 3:11 means. In this passage, the Holy Ghost says about God, "Before the mountains were brought forth, or ever thou hadst formed the earth and the world, even from everlasting to everlasting, thou art God." I looked up that word "everlasting" in this passage. (I always try to discover what a word means, and then I do not allow it to mean anything that it does not mean in the original.) So, in this case, the word "everlasting" twice used means, "from everlasting to everlasting God is God."

I find it fascinating that the Hebrew word for "everlasting" can have a variety of meanings. Often we see a word and assign it one particular definition where actually, it might have several. Such is the case with this word. I found that it can mean "time out of mind" or "always" or "to the vanishing point" or "to the beginningless past." To meditate on these meanings and reflect how they are found in God is to garner rich dividends in understanding God.

To contemplate God as He is, we must begin to see that He is "from time out of mind to time out of mind thou art God." We also begin to see, "Oh, God, from the always to the always thou remainest God." And then, "Oh, God, from the vanishing point out yonder down to the vanishing point out here, thou art God."

The application of all this that rises above human understanding is simply, "From the beginningless past to the endless future, thou art God."

How can we ever fully comprehend the everlastingness of God? It is not a matter of correct doctrine and theology here. Someone can have their doctrine down perfectly in a nice, neat package and yet fail to comprehend this matter of "everlastingness." Certainly I am not against doctrine and theology and understanding what the Bible teaches, but some things go beyond intellectual knowledge. John is pushing us and encouraging us to ascend into the rarified atmosphere of experiencing God in the wonderment of His everlastingness.

To ascend into the heart of God in this fashion is to begin to experience that Old Testament encouragement, "the eternal God is thy refuge" (Deut. 33:27). We find our finite harbored in that which has no beginning and no end. From a doctrinal point of view, we can passively accept the attributes of God and be fundamentally sound. We can say, "I believe in the eternity of God," and be on good footing theologically. But, oh, the wonder of a passage like this that transcends this kind of thing! To contemplate the thought, "Thou hast set the world in their hearts," and then to understand that we have been brought up into the eternity of God.

The Bible clearly teaches that God created man in His own image. Whatever that means, it must mean that there is something in God that responds to something in man.

The Holy Spirit has said this about the heart of man, whom God made in His own image: "He has put eternity into a man's mind" (*RSV*). That is it with a period. God says He has put "time out of mind" into the heart of a man. It says He has put the "everlasting beginningless" always into the heart of man.

Longing for Immortality

The reality that everywhere you go you see people who manifest a deep-seated restlessness shows that there is something deep within the soul, put there by God, that yearns for this everlastingness that is only found in God.

If we were of the earth only and belonged to the beasts, we would never be disturbed. There would never be much trouble in the world at all if God had not put everlastingness in us. Without everlastingness in the soul, I do not believe a Hitler or a Stalin would have tried to conquer Europe. But because of God's intentional design, there is in us an appreciation and a longing for the everlastingness of God. But we have lost it.

We wish we had it, and we want it; and we are dissatisfied with anything less.

Man, like an eagle in a cage, owns the cage and then drops back and forth from one war to another war. He goes from one strike to another strike, from one gamble to another gamble, from one dance to another dance, from one hell to another hell. Why do men act this way? Why do men and women fight against each other and strive for supremacy?

The answer is quite simple. God has buried something deep within the soul of every man and woman. It is simply and profoundly a longing for immortality. Although men and women know that everybody dies, they never think that they will die. When death approaches, they fight this enemy with all that is in them. Why? Because of that sense of immortality that God breathed into them when He breathed into Adam and he became a living soul.

What is true among men is rarely found in the animal kingdom. Nowhere among the creation do you find the corruption and downright meanness that we see in every city in our country. Why do the serpents under the rock and the whales in the sea and the beasts of the jungle manage to get along and kill only when necessary to eat? Then they lie down, sleep and wait for the night to come. Why do the beasts of the forest get along better than people? Why do they have less trouble? Why are they more moral?

I have no hesitation in saying that there is not a dog in Chicago that is less moral in many regards than his master, if indeed you can attribute morality to that which has not eternity in its heart. They live better and are more decent. Some people miss the significant difference between a man and an animal. Although a Christian may not subscribe to the theory of evolution, he may not see a significant difference between the man in the garden and the beast in the field. Often people compare the two. They might say, "That man is acting like a beast." But never have I heard somebody say, "That beast is acting like a man." No beast of the field is ever a target of Satan's attack. However, because God has put within the heart of each person a sense of everlastingness, man is the target of the devil's hateful attacks.

If we had more courage, we would preach more on the image of God in man. That does not mean that unconverted man is saved. He specifically is lost, and except he repent and be born again, he will never see the kingdom of God. If he dies unshriven and unforgiven, he will certainly go to hell. All that I believe, and the only reason a man can be saved is that God has put eternity in his heart. God made man in His own image, and though man fell, he keeps the longing after eternity there and the appreciation of everlastingness there. He has a desire after everlasting life within his heart, and that upsets him. Man goes wild and calls it one thing, but deep down in him it is another thing that is bothering him.

An Unnatural Atmosphere

God has assigned to everything natural responses. For example, it is quite natural for a bird to fly in the air. When somebody sees a bird flying in the air he doesn't say to the bird, "You should not be flying in the air. It's unnatural." The matter is, there is nothing more natural in all the world than for a bird to fly from tree to tree. There is nothing unusual about this. Every living thing has certain attributes that are natural to it.

In fact, we recognize animals and birds by their natural attributes. We are not surprised by the barking of the dog, the meowing of the cat or the sweet song coming from the bird of the forest. They are simply doing what comes natural to them.

Now enter the human scene. There are likewise natural responses or attributes. When a man begins praying to God, he is doing that as a natural response. God put into him that desire. Deep inside the heart of a man are responses that flow from him naturally. During the war, it was common to hear people say, "There are no atheists in foxholes." What that meant was that when the pressure was on and the bullets were flying, the soldier was reduced to his natural response—prayer. You can deny that natural response when far from the battlefield, but certain crises will bring it to the surface.

For that man or woman who has been redeemed by the blood of the Lamb, the most natural thing for that person is to lift his or her heart in prayer and praise to God. God put that response there, and redemption unleashes its capacity. This inward longing after mortality that every human experiences was established in the heart by God from the very beginning. When man fell in the Garden, it brought a dark cloud over the soul of mankind, suffocating him from the reality of immortality.

This suffocation is a terrible thing in the human race. The effects of this are seen in every jail, every hospital and every mental asylum in our country. People, created in the image of God, with the aspiration for immortality, are struggling under this suffocating cloud that hinders them in their pursuit of

God. The reality of this suffocation should tell us that something is wrong.

When I was a young boy living in the hills of western Pennsylvania, the men worked in the coal mines. Not only was it hard work, but also rather dangerous. Without all of the advanced technology we have today, coal miners had to improvise in many ways to be alert to danger. One method had to do with the level of air in the coal mine. They could never be sure when the air turned poisonous, so they would have caged birds down in the mineshaft. They knew how delicate those birds were; and when the air turned poisonous, the little birds would be the first to suffocate, thus giving warning to the men to get out of there.

A little bird could not live in that atmosphere. And I believe that is the way it is with the soul of a man. Man was created to soar into the heights of eternity and fellowship with God. God made him to look back on the everlasting vanishing point that was, and on into the eternal vanishing point that will be and feel no age nor count birthdays, but like God, live in God. But sin has ruined us. We have listened to that old serpent, the devil, and have gone down into the dark, gas-infested bowels of the world where men are dying everywhere of suffocation.

We were made to breathe the air of righteousness and everlastingness. In man's revolt against God, he brought upon himself this suffocating cloud that keeps him from being what God wants him to be and possessing what God desires him to possess.

Marks of the Counterfeit

Certain marks of this curse rest upon everything. "There is none that doeth good, no, not one" (Ps. 53:3), and with every good there is some evil lurking there. And under every beautiful thing, there is a coiled serpent.

As a lad, early in the spring, before the sun had thawed everything, I went out poking around in the woods and found a funny object that looked like a rag rug. But this object looked like a tiny rag rug, flat, rather pretty and neatly done. So I picked it up. It was about the size of a little saucer, and I took it home and said, "Look what I found . . . isn't this a pretty thing? It's flat, and it's just like one of these braided rugs." It began to get warm in the house, and I will give you three guesses what I had brought home. A snake! It had curled up and gone to sleep. It had wrapped around itself and had been so careful and made itself pretty for the winter. But it was still a snake; and as soon as it warmed, it uncoiled.

My proposition is simply this: Everything is wrong until Jesus sets it right. But you say, "Surely there's something good somewhere." There are those who will argue the universal goodness of mankind. But the truth does not support that assumption.

The truth is, everything has been tainted. The kiss of death rests upon everything in our world. Nothing in this world will help anybody toward God. Isaac Watts (1674–1748) asked this question in one of his hymns: "Is this vile world a friend to grace, to help me on to God?" The answer, of course, is no.

There is a battle royal between the brain and the heart. The brain makes one assumption and the heart completely disavows it. The brain revels in every modern advancement while the heart says, "that won't satisfy." The brain cries out for improvement while the heart cries out for everlastingness. The heart will never be satisfied with the desires of the brain. The heart was made for everlastingness while the brain is suffocating under the cloud of depravity.

In your home, you have a lovely modern stove. You set it to what you want it to do and then go shopping. When you come back, the food has finished cooking. It took grandma a day and a half to do what your stove does in a few minutes all by itself without you even watching it. Your animal nature says, "That's progress. That's wonderful!" But deeper down, if you listen, you will hear a quiet voice saying, "Oh no! That isn't it! That's not wonderful, that is temporal. That is recent, that is transient; that belongs for one brief day." It will not be long before other improved gadgets will replace the ones you are in love with now. And this vicious cycle will go on and on and on without any end in sight. In the light of all of this, we think we are progressing and we think we have it better than our forefathers.

Many people are caught up with the toys of contemporary society. Because of great advancements in our culture, some have cultivated an attitude of "comfortability." They may be going to hell, but it is going to be a comfortable ride for them.

Your poor heart, in which God put appreciation for everlastingness, will not take electronic gadgets in lieu of eternal life. Something inside of you is too big for that, too terrible, too wonderful. God has set everlastingness in your heart. All the things of this world are here for but a moment and then are gone. None can satisfy the longing for that eternal ragging in the soul of every man.

A Search for the Everlasting

The things of this world are transient. They are born for but a brief day. It may be something we like and that we think is wonderful. But the problem is, everything we enjoy is fleeting. The passing parade is here today and gone in a brief moment. Once the parade is gone, we look around for something else to take its place. But everything is temporary and provides only brief entertainment.

It seems to me that everybody is fascinated by some kind of toy. The problem is that the toy is so fragile that they can only enjoy it for a moment. The average person goes from one toy to the next toy.

A man will have a midlife crisis and acquire an old car with a souped-up engine full of noise and fire. By some trick of psychology, he imagines that the noise and power of that car makes him more than what he really is. In his imagination, he thinks if he gets in a big car, he is a big man. When he gets into the car, the deep rumble of that gorgeous motor makes him feel that he is a man at last—until a cop that never went past the fifth grade pulls him over and lectures him like he is a schoolboy. He experiences a temporary lift of his personality when he gets in that car, but he does not know that he is only allowing his deep soul, into which God has put eternity, to weep itself to death inside. He pays no attention to the cry after God and to the immortality that lies inside.

Modern women have every convenience imaginable and believe they are finally getting somewhere. They have it better than their grandmothers, but they are not getting anywhere, at least spiritually. Inside is something bigger than curls and plucked eyebrows, nylon and silk and fine-tooled leather. Bigger than a lovely home, a ranch-style house, a garage and a car, bigger than anything the world can give them. Something cries inside—the voice of God crying out for everlastingness and eternal life, deliverance and hope—but they are smothering it under house duties, longing for one thing and another. How foolish we mortals are.

That great something inside of me that appreciates everlastingness will not be satisfied without it. It cries, "That's what I wanted!" Not religion, not philosophy, not civilization—all those are too recent. My animal nature wants something recent, but my deep heart wants something eternal. Therefore, God says, "I made you that way, and now I have what you want: the Word made flesh to dwell among you. And he that receives Him, to them I give the power to become the sons of God, even to them that believe on His name." It's like a shipwrecked sailor floating on a raft, and looks and sees solid land and shouts his joy through parched lips. He has found something solid and knows that he will soon be on it.

Civilization, religion and everything man has devised have only betrayed humanity. We know that we are afloat, and we know that we are ready to perish. Then comes the Holy Ghost and says, "In the beginning was the Word, and the Word was with God, and the Word was God." There is eternity; and eternity "was made flesh, and dwelt among us . . . [and] whosoever believeth in him should not perish, but have everlasting life" (John 1:13; 3:16).

I do not go to the modernist and apologize. I do not go to the liberal and excuse myself. I do not go to the philosopher and say rather apologetically, "I'm sorry, but I'm a Christian." Rather, I go to these and say, "I have what you're looking for. This is what you need. Something in your heart was made to appreciate everlastingness and it will never be satisfied until it gets eternity and immortality and the promise thereof." And I say, "Now, I have it."

Paul went to Athens and to Corinth among the learned philosophers of his day and said, "For I determined not to know any thing among you, save Jesus Christ, and him crucified" (1 Cor. 2:2). That is the Rock, which is why we sing, "Rock of Ages cleft for me; let me hide myself in Thee." It is the Rock that lasts. The shipwrecked man is on the Rock now and is not going to perish. The Rock is solid. He may tremble and shake, but the Rock never shakes.

Where Christianity Starts

Every religion in the world had a beginning. You can trace it starting with its founder. All these religions have a beginning and they all have an ending. Christianity is different. Where does Christianity start? It has no beginning and it has no end. The human heart wants that which had no beginning and never can have any ending—namely, the Word, which was with the Father in the beginning; the Word, which was God; and the Word, which *is* God. Oh, how wonderful that God gives us this, and yet how terrible that many will not accept it! How terrible that we have to be frightened into heaven and whipped into it with the threat of hell!

The sin in our animal nature has ruined us. But oh, that we might turn unto God and Christ and say, "Lord Jesus, I believe

You! I believe that You are the Eternal Word and that in You I have the everlastingness that is equal to God's everlastingness. I have that eternal life which was with the Father." The life that God offers us is not a question of duration. It is a question of quality, and the quality of life that God gives us is His own life in your heart. That takes care of the duration and everything else.

God created our souls to be satisfied only with the divine everlastingness of the Word made flesh.

2

A TIME BEFORE
TIME BEGAN

*All things were made by him; and without him was not any thing made
that was made. In him was life; and the life was the light of men.*

JOHN 1:3-5

I want to ask you to do something virtually impossible, equiva-
lent to standing in a basket, reaching down, taking a hold of
the handles and lifting yourself up on the table. That would be
impossible; and what I am intending to ask would be impossible, except that when God made the human mind, He made a
wonderful, flexible and resilient instrument capable of doing
things that cannot be done.

While it would be impossible physically for you to stand in
the basket and lift yourself onto the table, it is not impossible
for you to do what I intend to ask. Moreover, I am going to pay
a compliment to your intellect to believe that you can do it, and
then I am going to have confidence in your spiritual hunger to
believe that you want to do it.

I am going to ask you to think everything out of existence.
Dismantle the universe, take it down stone upon stone, hurl it

into nothing and unmake everything that is made. In doing this, I will not be acting the part of the fool or playing with the truth, but I will only be trying to get back to where this text begins. I want you to think away everything with which you are familiar.

I want you to begin with this rolling stream we call "time." I want you to deliberately get hold of the handles of the basket, lift yourself up and say to yourself, "There was a time when time was not." Because our language is so limited, we have to use a word that we are trying to get rid of to tell you to get rid of the word. We will have to say that we want you to think of a time when time was not.

I then want you to think away space. In former days, a half-mile was quite a distance, and two miles was a real journey for an old horse and buggy. Now we get around rapidly. But I want you to think this away: I want you to dismantle the idea and break it down and get it out of your head and say there is no space. Then, there is no such thing as matter—with one of its attributes being impenetrability. I strike it with my knuckles and it stops me. That is matter. It has many forms, but think of the timeless time before space was, when there was no matter.

Now, think away all created things, and then think yourself away. Go back to the void, and then think the void away. To aid this, you will need to get into a rocket ship and race backward, not in space, but in time. In racing backward in time, you will get rid of many things, and the latest things will disappear first. Just as when you get in an airplane and soar upwards, the closest things necessarily are the ones that disappear first; and then as you go up and up, you see only the general skeletal outline of things down below.

Think away every city. Then think out of existence every bridge, every highway, every famous hotel, every ship, every train and every automobile. In addition, think back through the years to the time when Columbus discovered America and there was not anybody over here but Indians. They had this entire land, which we call the North American continent, from Hudson Bay country to the Rio Grande. Then think back to the day when Abraham walked in Ur of the Chaldeans, and on back to when there was just Adam and Eve. Now go back beyond Adam and Eve and think them out of existence.

By now, you are getting to the place where there is absolutely nothing in existence. But actually, you are only to the place that precedes time.

God Has No Beginning and No End

God had no beginning, because "beginning" is a creature word and means that someone was working on something. God started to work on it; He worked awhile and finished it. And it had a beginning and a "finish," and that is a creature word. But God is not a creature. God is the Creator; so you never can say that God had a beginning. God could not receive anything from anybody, because God had all there was. Get back of it all, to where God was, and discover that God is the uncaused one.

As the uncaused one, God is absolutely self-sufficient in Himself and needs nothing from anyone. From some of the appeals I have heard from pulpits across the country you would think God was in some desperate straits, needing an immediate bailout. From some appeals people might be tempted to say, "Poor God's in bad shape and no doubt there's a depression in heaven; but if I give faithfully, I'll save God's face and I'll bail God out." How utterly fantastic and far from reality! How in the world could a mere mortal rescue He who is immortal?

God does not need your money; and if you want to keep it and let it rust and ruin you, keep it. But do not think that if you give it you are doing God a favor. There is absolutely nothing anybody has that God needs. "If I were hungry, I would not tell thee: for the world is mine, and the fulness thereof" (Ps. 50:12).

Self-sufficient

God's self-sufficiency simply means that He needs nothing outside of Himself. For God to suffer a need of any kind would disqualify Him from being God.

Never imagine that the archangels, seraphim and angels in heaven are God Almighty's little helpers that He created in order to help Him get along, as a farmer might hire 10 men to help him at harvest time so that he would not be stuck when the rains came.

God had Himself a wonderful, glorious time in creating the universe to admire and to admire Him. But God does not need anything, because when you give God anything, you only give what God gave you in the first place. Every gift anybody ever gave God never enriched Him by receiving it. And when God gives anything, He is never any poorer for giving it. If you give $10 out of $100, you have $90 left and you are $10 poorer. But when God gives anything, God does not lose it. He gives without separating Himself from it. He gives without loss, and He receives back without gain, because God is all and takes in everything so that He never received anything from anybody that He did not give first.

Self-existent

I am concerned with what the Bible calls "before the foundation of the world," so I will point out further that God does not need His creation. If He needed anything, He would not be omnipotent. If God needed strength, He would not be omnipotent; and if He was not omnipotent, He could not be God. And if He needed counsel, He could not be sovereign, because He therefore would not have His sovereignty. And if He needed wisdom, He could not be omniscient; and if He needed support, He could not be self-existent. God has to be utterly uncreated and self-existent. That is God.

We are so smothered under the little dust of grains that make up the world, time, space and organized matter that we are likely to forget that God once lived and dwelt and loved and existed without support, without help and without creation.

Poet and hymnist Fredrick W. Faber celebrates God's self-existence in these verses from "Have Mercy on Us, God Most High":

When heaven and earth were yet unmade,
When time was yet unknown,
Thou, in Thy bliss and majesty,
Didst live and love alone.

Thou wert not born; there was no fount
From which Thy Being flowed;
There is no end which Thou canst reach:
But Thou art simply God.

How wonderful creation is,
The work that Thou didst bless;
And, oh! what then must Thou be like,
Eternal Loveliness!

In the Beginning

When Scripture says, "In the beginning, God created," it does not mean in the beginning of God. It means at the beginning of the creation. "In the beginning of the creation, God made the heaven and the earth"; so that phrase, "in the beginning," does not mean the birth date of God Almighty. It means the time when God ceased to be alone and began to make time, space, creatures and beings. So God began to create.

Many people are simply confused with matter. Preachers getting up in the pulpit exasperate this confusion by saying, "We've got to fight this materialism." The good brother does not bother to explain what he means; he just takes for granted that everybody is on the same page as he is. However, people look around for the enemy but cannot find it because they do not know what materialism looks like; therefore, they do not know what the preacher is looking for.

The word "materialism" is simply a jargon phrase, and many people simply cannot identify it. All it means is this: We have accepted matter as the ultimate. Anything you can touch, smell, taste, handle, see and hear—anything that yields to the senses—is matter. There are those who say that is all there is; there is nothing else. "All this talk about God and spiritual life and spiritual beings is so much superstition. We are simply here in the world, and our bodies and minds and our chemical outfit within our body and our nerves is all there is to it."

That idea is materialism in its practical form and is what people mean when they say we have to fight materialism. It does not mean you're going to get up, grab a sword and run after a fellow named Material and cut him down. Rather, it means you have to start believing that "in the beginning, God," and that matter is only a creation of God.

Space and Time

God created everything, and everything has its purpose. If you examine creation around us, everything is dependent on everything else. Nothing stands on its own. Only God stands on His own. Everything is interrelated and subject to everything around it.

God created all the matter that is around us, but matter cannot stand alone. It needed some place to occupy, so God created what we call space; all matter is stored in some space.

Then God created time in which to make room for motion. Motion is dependent upon time, which is really the sequence of motion. Motion unfolds itself in sequential order. God created that order, and it is within the scope of time that things change.

One created thing led to another created thing, and every thing came together rather nicely. There is not anything in creation that is not necessary. This is the marvelous and wonderful wisdom of God.

Nobody ever has to be afraid of time. Time has never hurt anybody yet. Time is a medium in which change takes place. It is not time that makes a baby grow up; it is change. Things change; and in order to change, there has to be a sequence of change. There cannot be 2 before there is 1. And there cannot be 3 before there is 2; and there cannot be 5 before there is 4. They change in a sequence, and that sequence is time.

Laws of the Universe

God Himself established the laws of all creation. These laws govern the way things behave. Nothing is left to chance, nor does anything carry out independent tasks without regard to everything else in the world. Everything in the universe operates like a well-oiled machine. Law governs time, space and matter, and that is about all there is to it.

That is simplifying it—perhaps oversimplifying it. Law is essentially God proclaiming, "Matter, you behave in a certain way." And to time, He said, "Now stretch out and let things move round; let there be sequence so babies can grow up and things can change and they won't always have to be sitting around in a rut."

God created life in order that life might be conscious of all of this—time, space, motion and matter. But this was not enough. In all of God's creation, there was nothing that was conscious of Him. There was nothing in the entire universe that could relate to God in a personal way.

God then created spirit, in order that there might be creatures conscious of Him. He organized the whole business and called it cosmos; and the result is the world around us today.

That, I know, is a simplistic way of stating the whole business, and to state it more in depth would take a series of complicated books explaining everything about our universe. Even then, it would fall short of really explaining that which God has done in the world around us, and the beginning of human thought.

Think of that beginning when all things began: back there in the beginning of the Gospel of John, the first chapter, first verse, first line, "in the beginning." That simple phrase depicts where time and matter and space began, where created life began, where law and order began, where history began.

When people refer to prehistoric times, they refer to what happened before man began writing. However, history did not begin when man first put something down on paper. A murder is committed. Two gangsters shoot each other, and that is history. It is not written up until the next day. It was prehistoric in a sense that it happened before historians recorded it for the front page of the newspaper. When we talk about anything being prehistoric, we only mean that it is prior to any written record.

Look at the Scripture here. I want to give you a little baptism of prepositions. I want to show you four prepositions having to do with "the beginning."

And, Thou, Lord, in the beginning hast laid the foundation of the earth; and the heavens are the works of thine hands (Heb. 1:10).

And he answered and said unto them, Have ye not read, that he which made them at the beginning made them male and female (Matt. 19:4).

For then shall be great tribulation, such as was not since the beginning of the world to this time, no, nor ever shall be (Matt. 24:21).

In the beginning was the Word, and the Word was with God, and the Word was God (John 1:1).

So we have: "in the beginning," "at the beginning," "since the beginning" and "from the beginning," and they all mean the same thing. They refer to a time when God dwelt alone and lived alone in uncreated majesty and glory. The Father in love with the Son; the Son in love with the Spirit; and the Spirit and the Father and the Son dwelling in the tranquility that had no beginning and can have no end. That marvelous, uncreated beauty of divine unity.

When God began to create, that was the beginning. "And, Thou, Lord, in the beginning hast laid the foundation of the earth; and the heavens are the works of thine hands" (Heb. 1:10). So when we learn about the foundation of the world in the Bible, we know that it means the beginning. A point when God started things.

Fellowship with the Infinite

As a youngster, when someone wanted to stop you, bring you up with a jar and make your teeth rattle, he would say, "Where did God come from?" When he said that, he would ask the question only a fool would ask, because he knew neither the Scriptures nor the power of God. The preposition "from" cannot apply to God, for the word "from" means that it was somewhere else and came here, whereas God is everywhere. Heaven and earth are filled with His glory, and God cannot come from anywhere. But all things come from God.

Notice in John 1:1-2 that "in the beginning was the Word, and the Word was with God, and the Word was God. The same was in the beginning with God."

It is hard for us to fathom a pre-creation void. However, there was no void. Some talk about that void between verses in Genesis chapter 1. But technically, there was no void, as we might understand it. The word "void" is a good and most useful word. It is a utilitarian word; and when you do not know what else to say, you say, "It is void." In pre-creation times, however, God was there, and God is all there is. God is the triune God, and back in that pre-creation time, the holy Trinity was busy with eternal mercies. God's mind was stirring with merciful thoughts and redemptive plans for humanity, so that we read in Ephesians 1:4, "According as he hath chosen us in him before the foundation of the world, that we should be holy and without blame before him in love."

This mystery defies explanation from a human standpoint. This mystery can barely be explained in terms of understanding. How is it that we were chosen in Him before the foundation of the world? How can we ever think of a time when we did not exist? How can we explain a time when there was no matter, no law, no motion, no relation and no space and no time and no beings, only God?

Then we encounter the foreknowledge of God, for it says in 1 Peter, "Elect according to the foreknowledge of God the Father, through sanctification of the Spirit, unto obedience and sprinkling of the blood of Jesus Christ: Grace unto you, and peace, be multiplied" (1:2).

Then there is, "Who verily was foreordained before the foundation of the world, but was manifest in these last times for you" (v. 20). "In the beginning, God created," but that was not God's first activity. God had been busy before that. Moreover, God had been busy in choosing and foreordaining from the beginning.

In Revelation 13:8, we read, "And all that dwell upon the earth shall worship him, whose names are not written in the book of life of the Lamb slain from the foundation of the world," and that was before Adam ever came into the world.

Some people's idea of God is quite disturbing to me. Somehow, they have the idea that God is like them only, of course, much better. They take their human attributes and project it up into God. As a result, they have a God, much like themselves, but a God I could never fall on my knees and worship. A God who does not deserve worship.

Consequently, when unexpected things happen to them and they find themselves in a real tether, they assume God experiences the same thing. I could never get on my knees and pray to a God I had to apologize for, or who desperately needed my help. A God who needs my help does not deserve my worship. If God needed me, I could not respect Him; and if I could not respect Him, I could not worship Him.

In this regard, missionary conventions are sometimes simply a session apologizing for God. Often the missionary challenge is reduced to: "Let's help God out because He needs us so bad."

The truth of the matter is that God is riding above this world, and the clouds are but the dust of His feet. If you do not follow Him, you lose, but God loses nothing. He still will be glorified in His saints and admired in all them that fear Him.

In that Great Day, that consummation of all that is called matter, law, time, space, angels, spirits and mind, all will be organized into a redeemed cosmos. Together, all that is redeemed will gather and sing and glorify God who made them and say, "Worthy is the Lamb that was slain to receive power, and riches, and wisdom, and strength, and honour, and glory, and blessing" (Rev. 5:12).

We should never come to God as a gesture of pity, thinking that God desperately needs us. We should give ourselves to God because He is worthy.

God has a hell prepared for people that do not want to serve Him—from the covering cherub that walked up and down the stones of fire, to the bishop or the pope or the pastor that would rather serve his own flesh and the devil than serve God. God—unsupported, unserved, needing nothing, dwelling in holy perfection; Father, Son and Holy Ghost—by the kind impulse of His own unstimulated heart—with no propaganda, no pressure, not even any prayer, but out of the impulse of His own heart—said, "I'll make Me a world."

And so He made the world, and then He said, "Now I've made it all, and now I'll make a being, that wondrous being capable of appreciating me, that the angels cannot even do, and I'll call him man and give him a mate, and I'll call her woman." So God made man in His own image, male and female made He them, and said, "Increase and multiply." God commanded man to increase and multiply so that the world will be filled with others that can gaze at the stars and say, "What is man that thou madest him?" That can kneel on his knees and say, "Our Father who art in heaven," and who can admire and worship and adore. That was out of the kindness of God, not out of any necessity laid upon Him. No greater being could lay a necessity upon Him. He did it because He wanted to do it.

Leave the morning newspaper unopened; just let the thing lie there. Do not turn the radio on to see who assassinated who; do not bother. Just think a little bit and say to yourself, before God, "I'm glad I'm alive. I am delighted that I was ever created. I am delighted that I was ever born. I am delighted that God ever thought of me before the beginning. I am utterly and completely delighted that God ever made me."

I remember reading Robert Burns's famous, funny poem "Tam o' Shanter." Tam o' Shanter was the Scotsman that rode a horse named Ole Meg. He was coming home from a wild party and feeling a bit high, and he passed an old church. The witches were dancing there and he was so taken with it that he got off Ole Meg and went and watched. They saw him and started after him and he jumped back on Ole Meg and started at a dead gallop across the water.

Back then it was thought that if you crossed running water, the witches could not follow you. One witch, a little livelier than the rest, was making time on Ole Meg, and just when their hoof beats were drumming over the wooden bridge, she grabbed Ole Meg's tail and with one mighty super-human bound, Ole Meg got loose; and after that, she had no tail, but at least she carried Tam to safety.

Some people have the idea that being saved is exactly that—to accept Jesus at the last jump, just before the devil gets you, leaving something behind maybe in the devil's hand, but thank God, breathless and panicked and covered with perspiration you get in at last. How utterly silly this whole business is.

God Almighty, before the beginning of the world, thought about you and planned your redemption. In those pre-creation times, God was thinking loving thoughts about you; and when you grieved Him by your sins, He still did not turn you over to hell. But a lamb slain from the foundation of the world came to save you and redeem you.

At conversion, you have only just started. When converted to Christ, you are a new creature. You have come up out of the old Adamic trash, you have crawled out of the wreckage by the grace of God and been made new. And God introduces you into His royal family and gives you of His Holy Spirit in an increasing measure.

Then begins that glorious growth upward and onward and that happy and holy pursuit of God that will never end. It all begins in conversion. It is greatly stimulated and accelerated when you are filled with the Holy Ghost. We will be further perfected in that glorious day when Jesus comes; and it will never end as long as God remains infinite and man remains finite.

The Only Thing that Truly Matters

I do not know what it all means to you, but it makes a place like Chicago pretty dirty to me. It makes money look like a pretty sordid thing to me. It makes the praise of man a cheap thing, and it makes me careless of whether anybody likes me or not—

whether they are willing to follow me or will not even come to hear me. I am pretty careless about the whole business. In light of eternity and the long, long thoughts of God, and the plans of everlastingness and perfection, and the consummation and the coming of Jesus, I wonder what it all matters.

Yet there are Christians in mortal fear of offending some carnal old fellow. They would not draw blood lest somebody would say they are fanatic. There never lived a good man in the entire world but some child of the devil did not say he was a fanatic. And there never was a holy testimony given by the breath of the Holy Ghost that somebody did not say the man was a fanatic. Some people had rather die than be called a fanatic.

In the light of eternity and the long, long reaches, I wonder if it matters very much what somebody thinks about you. Just down on a common political level, it did not make much difference what they thought about Abraham Lincoln. The ages have justified Abraham Lincoln. It does not make too much difference what they thought of Martin Luther, not too much.

So the Lord Jesus Christ is calling you out. If you were a heathen, I would have to explain, but I can only quote: "But these are written, that ye might believe that Jesus is the Christ, the Son of God; and that believing ye might have life through his name" (John 20:31).

Christ has every claim on you and me. Nobody knows what tomorrow will bring or even tonight or the next hour. But there walks One among us who walked among the ancient trees. There walks One among us who walked before the world was.

3

THE BEAUTEOUS WORLD AS MADE BY HIM

He was in the world, and the world was made by him,
and the world knew him not.

JOHN 1:10

The Gospel of John is so profound and highly packed with truth that I would affront the Spirit of Truth if I were to hurry through it. The phrase, "He was in the world, and the world was made by him, and the world knew him not" (John 1:10) cannot be rushed without dire consequences.

The pronoun "him" refers to that which is spoken of in John 1:1, "In the beginning was the Word, and the Word was with God, and the Word was God," and in verse 10, "He was in the world, and the world was made by him, and the world knew him not." All this refers to pre-incarnation times and does not refer to the coming of Christ at Bethlehem, but the world of humanity from its beginning.

We have the "Word" and the "world" related in this prologue as cause and effect. The "world" is always an effect, the "Word"

45

is always a cause, and there never is any time when the world is a cause, and there never is any time when the Word is an effect. The "Word" was and the "Word" made the "world." The *logos* (in English, the "Word") made the world, and we will stay by it. So the "Word" and the "world." The world you see round about you did not come into existence of itself but is an effect of that which the Bible calls the Word.

The word "world" needs a bit of definition, so I want to mention that the word "world" has three meanings in the Bible, only two of which concern us now. The third one means ages, but the prologue is not concerned with the ages as such. The prologue uses the word "world" in two of its meanings: nature and humanity. And it is the very same Greek word in both cases and used together without clear distinction; so when the Bible says, "He was in the world and the world knew Him not," you have two meanings of the word "world," and the context has to tell you which meaning it is, because it is a precise word in the original.

"World" as Nature

The word "world" comes from a root meaning: "to tend and to take care of and to provide for." This is obvious just from reading the Scriptures, even if we never looked in any Greek lexicon. It also means an orderly arrangement, plus a decoration.

Orderly

To the casual observer the world around us is an orderly world. I do not think I'm too wrong in referring to it as the monotony of order. Anyone can see that day follows night, winter follows summer and there has been no change since the beginning of time. God's world is a world that is orderly. This monotony of order is quite crucial to everything in nature. Without it all of nature would crumble in a pile of chaos.

A world of uncertainty would be uncharacteristic of God, for the Scriptures clearly state, "For God is not the author of confusion, but of peace, as in all churches of the saints" (1 Cor. 14:33). Wherever you see confusion, you can be sure that something is wrong. Disorder in the world implies that something is out of place. Usually, at the heart of all disorder you will find man in rebellion against God. It began in the Garden of Eden and continues to this day.

All of nature has come to expect from God a sense of orderliness. Whatever God does carries with it His fingerprint. And in the world around us His fingerprint of orderliness is evident to anybody who is honest with the facts. If you look at nature, you will discover a mathematical exactness. Without this precision, the entire world would be in utter confusion. One plus one always equals two no matter what part of the universe you happen to be in. And the laws of nature operate in beautiful harmony, a harmony that is ordered by God Himself.

Beautiful

Not only would we expect God to make an orderly world that operates in perfect harmony, but also a beautiful world. And it is not difficult to see that the world around us is full of beauty. When we look at the world, especially from that point of view, we cannot help but see the beauty. I once flew over the Grand Canyon and could not help but wonder at the marvelous beauty of God's creation. It brought to me a sense of awesome appreciation of God's creative prowess.

The hymn writers of the church have done a magnificent job of reminding us of God's beautiful creation. The words to "For the Beauty of the Earth" by Folliot Sandford Pierpoint (1835–1917) express this very thing:

> For the beauty of the earth,
> For the glory of the skies,
> For the love which from our birth
> Over and around us lies,
> Lord of all, to Thee we raise
> This our hymn of grateful praise.

The hymn writer was putting in melodious language a truth that God made the world beautiful in its order.

The reason God created the world as beautiful as it is, was to please Himself. Everything He created brought pleasure to Him in some way. We read of this in Revelation 4:11: "Thou art worthy, O Lord, to receive glory and honour and power: for thou hast created all things, and for thy pleasure they are and were created."

When we see any beauty, we must understand that it is simply being what it was created to be. God did not make anything ugly. I know that there are some strange creatures out in the world, but each one brings a certain degree of pleasure to the Creator. He created all of this for His delight. We can only imagine the enjoyment God gets out of some of the things that I have seen.

There is an old saying that we hear often: "Beauty is in the eye of the beholder." Could I be so bold as to change that a little bit and make it more biblically correct? "Beauty is in the eye of the Creator." That makes more sense to me. I have seen babies with a face only a mother could love. I don't say anything, because every baby is beautiful to its parents. Why? Well the answer is obvious. The parents see something of themselves in that little bundle.

When we come to God and His outlook on the world around us, what He sees is beautiful. The reason is simple. Everything God created, He created with purpose, and that purpose brings pure pleasure to Him. God looks at His marvelous creation and, in a sense, sees Himself.

When we think of something ugly, we think of something that is really out of place. And although, for the time being, there are some things in this world out of place and therefore ugly, God, who created all things, will make sure all things come back to their created purpose.

Every artist is in love with his creation because he puts something of himself into it. Others may not appreciate the beauty, but the artist sees what others may not see—what he intended to create.

The reason things are as out of place as they are is because of sin. When God created man and put him in the garden, everything was perfect. There was not a bit of ugliness anywhere to be found. And God looked at everything and pronounced, "It is good." The world God created, and the world in which God placed man, was perfect and good. It brought great delight and pleasure to the Creator.

Sin brought in disorder; and in that disorder was ugliness. It was a revolt against God and His creative purpose. To restore the beauty of God's world, God sent the Redeemer to put all things back to its creative purpose. Only the redeemed have the ability to like what God likes and to be pleased with what pleases God.

In the untouched beauty and majesty of God's creation, we begin to understand God's great appreciation of things beautiful. Only man's touch on God's creation taints it with ugliness.

Utilitarian

God's world is orderly and decorative, but it is also utilitarian. In examining God's creation, one simple thought I have is that nothing was made on whimsy. God is not like man who does things impulsively and then later has reason to regret what he has done. I have done things and later have come to regret them and found that there is no practical use whatsoever for what I have done.

Not so with God. Everything God does has purpose and intention behind that design. It is a master design, and every little thing has its proper place and function.

Just because I, finite man, do not understand everything that God, the infinite, does is no reason to doubt God's purpose. I may go into someone's workshop and see all the tools and gadgets that are important to the man's work. I may see laying on the table, for instance, a little tool that I can make nothing of and have no understanding of its purpose. But in the hands of the craftsman, that little tool has a well-defined purpose and does what it's supposed to do.

Just because the man's worktable looks cluttered and as if everything is out of place does not mean in his mind there is not order and purpose. In the same regard, I am not going to accuse God of creating a lot of unnecessary things that have no purpose in God's total scheme of things, just because I don't understand them.

I give you that sometimes it is difficult to find the utilitarian purpose of something. My father, for example, could not understand the purpose behind the mosquito. As far as he was concerned, it was an annoying little insect and had no purpose whatsoever. Yet I believe that everything has a well-defined purpose in God's creation. I may not understand it at the time, and it may look like something completely out of place with no purpose at all, but everything God does has at its very foundation a utilitarian purpose.

In the first part of the book of Genesis, we see that utility was God's first plan. God said, "Let there be light" (Gen. 1:3). And God saw that it was good, it had a purpose, and He divided the light from the darkness. The purpose of that was for utility. God called the light day and the darkness He called night. And everything we read in the first several chapters of Genesis show us a beautiful exercise in utility. God was making an orderly world for a purpose, giving a reason for its existence.

We must take this aspect of God's character and bring it over to the subject of men and women. This is exactly how people function. In the founding of our great country, the pioneers traveled west and hewed out for themselves homes. The first great purpose of those homes was utility. They were nothing to look at but were a shelter from the inclement elements. They served the purpose. And as it is everywhere, usefulness always comes first. That which God creates first has a utilitarian aspect to it. It has a specific purpose.

Decorative

After God created everything, He crowned it with His proclamation, "It is good." And to whom was it good? Simply put, what God saw was good in His own eyes. Not only did it have a utilitarian purpose, but it also was decorative. It not only satisfied His requirements for order and usefulness, but it was also well pleasing to His eye. First, God made a thing useful, and then He added decoration.

Something can be useful and look ugly. We can get some work out of it, but it still can be an awful-looking thing when it comes to aesthetics. God decorates everything He does with a wonderful sense of beauty. Everything God does is pleasing to His eye.

When God made His universe, it was just as easy for Him to make it lovely as it was to make it homely. Of course, it would have been useful even if the clouds above were square and painted battleship gray. They would be useful but they would never be nice to look at, and nobody would ever write a sonnet to a square cloud painted battleship gray. But the poets have written sonnets of the beautiful fleecy clouds that float in the blue sky above.

Why did God make the sky blue when any old color would do? God said, "That was a lovely color, wasn't it?" He liked it. He had something in Him that liked it. Then He made you and me, and there is something in us that likes it too.

In creation, God could have made a straight, plain, ugly-looking thing and called it a river. It would have worked, fed the fish and done all the things a river could do. But God in His gracious wisdom took His finger and traced the path of the river and allowed it to run around the tree and around the hills and down through a valley. He then surrounded it with beautiful trees, bushes and flowers. He also permitted it to catch the blue of the sky and reflect it as a beautiful mirror.

Utility is one thing and beauty is another, but God is able to make things both useful and beautiful. That is what the word "world" means.

"World" as Humanity

The first use of the word "world" is nature, and we can see how God has filled it with His presence. The second use of "world" is humanity. This does not refer to the clouds, the hills or the rocks in the rivers, but to the entire world of organized, fallen humanity. It is for this "world" that God sent His Son to redeem.

Before Christ came into the world, the world was a Shekinah of the Word, the all-permeating Word and will of God moving creatively throughout His universe. And when Jesus Christ became incarnate in human body, He did not cease to be the all-permeating Word filling the universe and moving among us. He did not cease ever to be what He always was and will be.

Now He is among us. He is the light "which lighteth every man that cometh into the world" (John 1:9). He now has come among the world of humanity.

Listen to this: "For by him were all things created, that are in heaven, and that are in earth, visible and invisible, whether they be thrones, or dominions, or principalities, or powers: all things were created by him, and for him" (Col. 1:16). The all-permeating Word, which is in the world, is the adhesive quality of the universe. That is why we do not fall apart. He is to the universe the mortar and the magnetism that holds it together. He holds up His universe. That is what He is doing in His universe. That is why He is here. This is not a dead world that we inhabit. Only sin is the dead thing. This is a living world that we inhabit, a spiritual world, held together by the spiritual presence of the invisible Word.

What is He doing? "Who being the brightness of his glory, and the express image of his person, and upholding all things by the word of his power, when he had by himself purged our sins, sat down on the right hand of the Majesty on high" (Heb. 1:3).

Why doesn't this world of ours just fall apart? What is it that holds everything together? Why doesn't the entire universe disintegrate into chaotic nothingness? The reason is, there is a presence making all things consist, and there is One upholding all things by the word of His power. Man in all of his educated smugness thinks he has the universe all figured out. He thinks he has boiled everything down to a scientific formula that he can prove or disprove whenever he chooses. The universe is in his hands. But this universe and all of nature are completely within the hands of God who is holding it all together.

It is of my distinct opinion that only spiritual laws can explain this universe. This is a spiritual world, which is why the scientist never manages to get through to the root of things. The educated scientist deals only with things he can see and touch and taste and experiment with, but he does not know why they hold together. He mixes two chemicals and a certain action takes place, and he writes about it and says, "Where is God?" God is making you do that. God is holding it together. The scientist says that a star in 2,510 years and 20 minutes will be in such and such a position. Then he says, "Now, I've done it. I have run God out of His world. I can predict where the stars will be." The scientist acts as though he has put those stars in the sky. Foolish man. The stars would never be anything but dust except God runs the whole show and did the whole business. God upholds all things by the word of His power.

What is God doing in His universe, this present, permeating *Logos*? "Lift up your eyes on high, and behold who hath created these things, that bringeth out their host by number: he calleth them all by names by the greatness of his might, for that he is strong in power; not one faileth" (Isa. 40:26). This is one of the most beautiful figures of speech in the entire Bible. I believe it is a companion piece to Psalm 23, only astronomical in place of dealing with human beings. The man of God said, "Lift up your eyes upon high and behold who has created these things."

What things? Those shining, bright diamond objects that look down upon the country and the city, their light reflecting off of the still water of the sea. Those stars embedded deep in the sky above. Who created those stars that bring out their host by number? Why do they bring out their host? To change the figure of speech a little, they are like sheep, and this is a figure of a shepherd bringing his sheep out by number and calling them all by name. Counting them as they come out, naming every one of them and leading them across the green grass of the meadows and beside the still waters. The shepherd-minded poet Isaiah saw the starry host above like a flock of sheep, and God, the great Shepherd, called them as they came sailing out through interstellar space as He numbered them and said they are all here and then called them by their names. And because He is strong in power, not one fails.

This is the most majestic and elevated figure of speech in the entire Bible, with no possible exception. We can look into the starry sky and know that astronomers have told us that the very Milky Way is not a milky way at all but simply a confusion of stars so many billions of light years away, all moving in an orderly direction. God called them all out and He knows their number and calls them all by name, just as a shepherd calls his sheep.

A Presence and a Light

In our country, we have a tradition of believing that there is a divine law in this world. Benjamin Franklin, who was not what we would call a fundamentalist Christian, suggested that when the Congress was in a tight spot, they should stop everything and have prayer. Many of them really were not Christians, but they believed in God. They believed there was a God in this world and that there was a divine law in the world. This was the foundation of our country.

Although our founding fathers were not fundamental Christians, and many were not born again, most of them held a reverent and profound belief in the presence of God in this world. All of the laws and rules and regulations that have come down to us from them came from men who believed there was a God. That did not save them, but it made them a lot different from many today who scoff at the idea of God. Today in Washington and other places there are those whose idea of God is so cynical that they might toss God somewhere in their speeches but their entire life is lived as though He didn't really exist.

When you get up in the morning, there is a presence, and you do not feel it. There is a light, and you do not see it. You get up in the morning, and there is a voice, but you cannot hear it, and then you say, "Don't preach to me, go preach to the down-and-outers on skid row." Don't you know that before the great bar of God, your sin is deeper than the drug addict lying in the cool of the alley in some gutter?

Others are addicted to pleasure and give themselves to the pleasures of the flesh—anything to take the seriousness out of living. Anything to keep from knowing that there is a presence. Anything to keep from knowing there is a light and a voice.

You may dress in expensive suits and drive the latest automobile; your home may be more than you can really afford and not one thing in it more than a year old. You may have promotions coming up and expect to make good in this world. But you are a profane man until you have awakened to the fact that you are not alone in this universe, but He is here. That there is a presence and a voice that lights every man, and you realize the basis of your life is not physical but spiritual, and you owe it to God to turn to Him with all your heart.

It is a tremendous thought that when our Lord wanted to point to the most dangerous trap of all, He did not mention the wicked things. He said the most dangerous trap is just living and forgetting that God exists.

This is what is wrong with America. Any kind of sin will damn any man that does not get free from it by the blood of the Lamb.

It is noteworthy that Jesus Christ specializes in talking about these innocent things that are all right in themselves, but when we get absorbed in them to the point where there is a presence and we cannot feel Him, a voice and we cannot hear Him, a light and we cannot see Him, then we are profane men. "Let the day perish wherein I was born, and the night in which it was said, There is a man child conceived. Let that day be darkness; let not God regard it from above, neither let the light shine upon it" (Job 3:3-4).

The only Scripture for that profane man who has forgotten Jesus Christ exists is, "He was in the world, and the world was made by him, and the world knew him not" (John 1:10). The man has a responsibility to God—God made him; he is an effect, not a cause, an effect of a cause. And he is in the hand of God, if he only knew it. God will send him into hell because he has forgotten that there is a God. He gives lip service to the church and mental service to religion, but he is a profane man because he cannot see the presence or the light or hear the voice that says, "Come unto me, all ye that labour and are heavy laden, and I will give you rest" (Matt. 11:28).

I can but offer my own personal testimony. As a 17-year-old ignorant boy walking the streets of east Akron, I wandered into a church and heard a man say, "Come unto me, all ye that labour and are heavy laden, and I will give you rest. Take my yoke upon you, and learn of me; for I am meek and lowly of heart: and ye shall find rest unto your souls" (Matt. 11:28-29).

I did not have any biblical background whatsoever. I, basically, was nothing more than a pagan; but when I heard those words, I was disturbed to my very soul. I began to feel a presence. I began to think I heard a voice and dimly saw a light. Although I was still a lost pagan, I was getting close. Jesus said, "Thou are not far from the kingdom of God" (Mark 12:34).

It was not long after that, when walking down Market Street, that I came to Case Avenue at the bottom of the hill and saw a street preacher. I still can see him in my mind. He was German, and spoke with a strong German accent and had a berry-colored birthmark disfiguring the side of his face. He was not much to look at but what he said burned deep into my heart: "If you don't know how to pray, go home and pray 'God, have mercy on me a sinner.'" Do you know what? I did it. I got into my Father's house and got my feet under the table.

Just get down on your knees. There is an awful lot you do not need to know to find God. The light shineth, the voice calleth and the Presence is here. All of this came to a head when Scripture says, "And the word was made flesh, and dwelt among us," and, "His glory, the glory as of the only begotten of the Father" (John 1:14); so He's here now. He went away in His human body, but His everlasting all-permeating Word is with us still.

4

THE TRAGIC SIDE OF CHRIST BECOMING FLESH

He came unto his own, and his own received him not.

JOHN 1:11

We often talk of how marvelous it was that God came in the flesh, dwelt among us and walked among us. It certainly was filled with marvel and mystery, but there is a side of His coming that is more tragic than the skills of a William Shakespeare could ever portray.

These two words, "He came," have a marvelous fascination for me. In the beginning of John's Gospel, we discover what Christ was doing before the creation of the world. John uses some very simple words: "He was," "in Him was," "He was with," "He was God," "He was in." Although these are very simple words, they are the root of theology and the root of all truth. Then in John 1:11, for the first time, we are given a suggestion of the Incarnation. "He came"; that is the first indication. Before that, it had been in the eternal past or it had been since the creation but before the Incarnation. "In Him was life," "in the beginning He was," "in the beginning He was God," "all things were made by Him; and without him was not any thing made that was made," and "that was the true Light, which lighteth every man that cometh into the world."

I cannot get away from the wonder of these words, "He came." The story of pity and mercy and redeeming love are all here in two words: "He came." All the pity that God is capable of feeling, all the mercy that He is capable of showing and all the redeeming grace that He could pour out of His heart are at least suggested here in two simple words: "He came." All the hopes and longings and aspirations and dreams of immortality that lie in the human breast had their fulfillment in those two words.

I wonder if that should not suggest to us that simplicity is always best and that you can say more with short words than with long ones. And that brevity beats the interminable pouring out of verbiage preachers are given to. It says, "He came," and with it all the hopes of humanity; man has always been a hopeful creature.

In his *Essays of Man,* Alexander Pope wrote, "Hope springs eternal in the human breast, Man never is, but always to be blest." He caught the essence of that which is always present in the human breast. Man at his worst, on his worst day, groveling in the dirt and lying in the pigsty, possesses a heart that aspires to better things. The prodigal son who is in the pigsty remembered his father's house and said, "What am I doing here?" He may lie there and never get up, but he aspires, he remembers. And the entire human race has dreams of immortality.

Nobody wants to hear, "The remains of so-and-so will be at Lane's undertaking establishment." There is something in us that fights death to the bitter end. Our minds will not accept it. Everybody knows they are going to die, but they do not believe they are going to die. Mentally they cannot visualize it and will not surrender to it. All humanity harbors hopes of immortality and dreams of a life to come. Where did this dream come from? Why does it pervade all of humanity? Very simply, we have been created in the image of Christ. Buried deep within our created soul is the echo of immortality. And all of this is summed up here in these two, one-syllable words, "He came," which occupy only seven spaces on the line; and yet what He tells us here is more profound than all philosophy.

Gather together in one place all the great philosophy of every culture from the beginning of time and none of it remotely approaches the wonder and profundity of the words "He came."

Highly underrated, these words are more beautiful and eloquent than all oratory, more musical than all music and more lyrical than all song, because they tell us that we, who are in darkness, were visited by the Light. I wish that when we sing, "The light of the world is Jesus," we could get a look on our faces that would make the world believe we mean it. I wish we would get as thrilled about it as they were in those early times.

John Milton celebrated the coming of Jesus into the world in his poem "On the Morning of Christ's Nativity," one of the most beautiful odes ever written:

This is the Month, and this the happy morn
Wherin the Son of Heav'ns eternal King,

Of wedded Maid, and Virgin Mother born,
Our great redemption from above did bring;
For so the holy sages once did sing,
That he our deadly forfeit should release,
And with his Father work us a perpetual peace.

That glorious Form, that Light unsufferable,
And that far-beaming blaze of Majesty,
Wherwith he wont at Heav'ns high Councel-Table,
To sit the midst of Trinal Unity,
He laid aside; and here with us to be,
Forsook the Courts of everlasting Day,
And chose with us a darksom House of mortal Clay.

That was Milton's description of the Incarnation, and I delight in the beauty of his portrayal.

Although "He came" carries with it the fascination and delight that is beyond any description, John then says, He came unto "His own." As rich and beautiful as the first phrase is, this takes it one step further. The two words "His own" are the same in our English, and yet they are utterly and completely different as used by John. The first "His own" is translated "His own things," "His own world," "His own home." "He came unto His own world." "He came into His own possession." "He came unto His own things." One translation says, "He came unto His own home but His own people received Him not." So that "His own," as used in the second place, does not refer to the same thing used in the first place. "He came to His world and His own people didn't know who He was and didn't receive Him."

The assumption here is, "He came unto His own world." For this is Christ's world. This world we buy, sell, kick around, lord over and take by force of arms—this world is Christ's world; He made it and He owns it all.

Some people make a great deal about God being "our honored guest tonight." Or even some go so far as to say, "God is our senior partner." This, of course, is utterly ridiculous. Those who claim God as their senior partner run their business as they see fit while their name is over the door. Our Lord Jesus Christ is not a guest here; neither is He anybody's "senior partner." He is the one that owns all things.

Around Christmastime, people say nice things about the baby Jesus. Even the secular news media will fawn over the Christ child very patronizingly. Christ does not need our patronage and He needs no one to act as His public-relations man. He is not a guest, He is the host and we are the guests. We are here by His sufferance. We are here by His kindness. We are here because He has made us and brought us here. And this world is His world, and He can do what He will with His world, and no one can upbraid Him. He can do what He wills with life and death and nature. And He can do what He wills in that mighty cataclysmic time that we call judgment.

Strange as some people may think of this, the Lord Jesus Christ does not need our defense, nor do we need to apologize for Him. He is quite capable of defending Himself and speaking for Himself. The God who needs our defense does not deserve our worship. The One who created all things, including the ground on which we stand and build our temporary buildings, does not need anybody running around apologizing for Him.

Nor does He need anybody rushing in taking His part and saying, "Now just a minute, He doesn't mean that. He sent judgment upon Sodom and Gomorrah but it doesn't quite mean that, it means something else." It means exactly that, and when God Almighty turned Lot's wife into a pillar of salt, it meant exactly that. And when the Bible tells us there is a hell where the wicked are going, it means exactly that. It does not mean something else.

God does not need me, or anybody else for that matter, to stand up and make excuses and try to explain in such a way that the world will understand. My business is to come crawling to His feet, a sinner filled with sores, and say, "Touch me and make me whole." And I stand up on my feet and look into the heavens and say, "I was once a sinner, but now I'm redeemed, and the Lord has saved me, and now I'm His child and I can keep my chin up."

God made this world in which we live, and so it is His world. If I am a Christian, then this is my Father's world. It belongs to the Trinity. It is not mine, and I live here by the good grace of God. Everything I handle and touch belongs to my Father. All the air and winds and the clouds and the corn and the waving wheat and the tall, noble forests and flowing rivers—they are all His.

G. Campbell Morgan, in his book *The Crises of the Christ*, points out that many people have a wrong conception of Jesus in the wilderness. When Jesus went into the wilderness to be tempted of the devil, He was there 40 days and 40 nights and was with the wild beasts. Morgan said that there was a wrong conception about that. We pitied Him and wondered how He could ever stand it to be with the wild beasts, and thought that those wild beasts might have wanted to attack Him, and He had to have angelic protection.

Campbell Morgan said properly, "No, it was not true." The wild beasts recognized their King and they crept to His feet, licked them, no doubt, and lay down beside Him. They recognized their Lord and Maker, and the very tawny lion shook his mane and kneeled beside His Savior, and the very bear that might have devoured another man knelt and whined at the feet of the man who was fasting 40 days and 40 nights.

Instead of pitying Jesus for those terrible hours or days spent with the wild beasts, we ought to remember that He was perfectly safe there, for not a sharp claw would tear the skin of the man who was God. And not a fang would rip the body of the man who was God. The very wind blew for His pleasure. He waxed and grew in body and wisdom; the very earth on which He trod smiled; the stars at night looked down on His humble carpenter cottage; and the winds and the rains and the snow were all His strength. He was in harmony with nature. The natural world was not against Him, only the human world.

As a Christian, it is entirely possible to be more in harmony with nature than the unsaved world. Saint Francis of Assisi was in harmony with nature, and the world has wondered at him. Some have laughed, some have scoffed and others have raised their eyebrows and wondered if he was in his right mind. But Saint Francis was so completely yielded to God and so completely in-filled and taken up by the presence of the Holy Ghost that all nature was his friend.

Scripture says, "the stars in their courses fought against Sis-era" (Judg. 5:20). And if the stars in their courses fought against the enemy, then those same stars in their courses fought in fa-vor of the friend of God. I believe it is so possible to be so tuned to God that the very stars and their courses are on our side. And nature smiles and owns their King. And God, when He made Adam, said, "Now you be over the whole business," and sin came in and wrecked it all. When sin is removed, I can understand why Saint Francis could preach to the birds and call the wind and the rain his friends, and the moon his sister, and live a de-lighted life because God's blessed world received him.

Look at humanity today and see how many are burdened with a deep sense of shame. What are we ashamed of? What is it about us, who were created in the image of God, to be ashamed of? Only one thing. That one thing is sin. It is not the world that God created; because if you were to take sin out of the world there wouldn't be anything to fear or be ashamed of.

There would never be another sick person in the world; no-body would be a victim of some vicious crime; there would not be a criminal behind any bars or any insane person living in an insane asylum.

There would not be any evidence anywhere of evil. If you took sin out of the world, you could leave your house unlocked. You could carry your money around in your pants pocket and not have to put it in a bank behind bars with a cop to watch it. And we could walk anywhere in the city and not be afraid of being attacked, if we could only take sin out of the world.

In the Gospel record, we see that Jesus was never sick an hour, and nothing was ever wrong with Him. He carried a perfect body to Calvary; and although He bore our sicknesses, they were poured on Him. God Almighty took all that swill barrel of bubbling, crawling, vicious, venomous juice called sin and poured it on the body of Jesus. He died under our sins and under our sicknesses, but He never had any sin and He never had any sickness.

Why His Own Received Him Not

Any student of history can easily point out some of the great blunders of all time. It would not be hard to point out the greatest moral blunder in the history of the world, which was when Christ came to His own world—the world that received Him not. He came to His own people, and His own people rejected Him. The very caterpillar on the leaf received its King; but the Jews, His own people, turned Him away.

The Bible speaks that blindness: "Go, and tell this people, Hear ye indeed, but understand not; and see ye indeed, but perceive not. Make the heart of this people fat, and make their ears heavy, and shut their eyes; lest they see with their eyes, and hear with their ears, and understand with their heart, and convert, and be healed" (Isa. 6:9-10). Moral and spiritual blindness lay upon them and they did not recognize Him. It was a stroke of God Almighty upon them for sin and they did not recognize it.

Why didn't His own receive Him? The natural world received Him because He was the God of creation, but humanity did not receive Him.

There were five reasons why His own rejected Him and why people even today reject Him.

A Change in Priorities

The first reason for rejecting Christ has to do with personal priorities. To receive Jesus when He was here in the world would have meant possible financial loss. We have an example in the rich young ruler (see Matt. 19:16-29). For him to follow Jesus would mean losing every bit of his property, for the Lord told him to go and get rid of it. And the people of Jesus' day would not receive Him because they loved their money more than they loved their God.

Why do people not receive Him today? The answer is simple and yet complicated. In order to receive Jesus Christ as He demands to be received requires turning your back on everything, which might mean personal financial loss. Some people, if they ever would want to follow Jesus Christ, would have to turn their back on and get out of a rather lucrative business. But you say, "I don't think so. I think they can just glorify God where they are." I admit there is a lot of that going on now. No matter what you are doing, you cannot just say, "I am a Christian," and begin to testify where you are.

To accept Jesus Christ means absolutely no compromising with the world.

I have suggested that if things keep on going from bad to worse in evangelical circles, the time will come pretty soon when we'll print John 3:16 at the bottom of a beer mug so that when a fellow drains it and looks at the bottom he will see salvation shining out at him. And halfway houses will have text that the girls give out with their favors. Some things you cannot do and be a Christian, and you might as well settle that now.

The Old Testament Jews wanted to do what they wanted to do, and they rejected Jesus because they knew they could not do what they wanted to do if they received Him. And there are people with all this revelation and all this light and information and yet they will not receive Him who the very angels and stars and rivers receive. Because they know they will have to give up something; it will mean financial loss.

A Change of Habit

The second reason has to do with our habits. For the Jews, to receive Jesus Christ would have meant a change in their way of living. They refused to allow the pattern of their life to be disturbed. Their habits were firmly established and nobody was going to change them.

This carries through today. To receive Jesus Christ will mean a change in our way of living. Some people are not going to change their way of living, no matter what. They will go underground. I am sure that is all my preaching does to some people. It just drives them underground. Occasionally, I shell the woods to drive these people out into the open. For the most part, they plug their ears and go deeper underground. But they do not change their ways any, and God knows they do not change their ways. They just go underground, and it is just as bad to be underground sinners as it is to be overt sinners.

Personal Cleansing

The third reason for refusing Christ had to do with their personal cleansing. Accepting Christ would have meant a thorough inward housecleaning. Jesus taught that the pure in heart would see God and the mourner would be comforted and the meek would have the earth and the merciful would be blessed.

This reason keeps many out today. Before Christ will come in there must be a thorough, if not radical, housecleaning.

One thing you can be sure about that manger in Bethlehem, it was clean. Mary did not have her baby in a dirty manger. It was not the fanciest or most elegant of places, but it was clean. It was simple; it was plain; it was crude. But it was clean. They put fresh straw down for that event; don't you think they didn't. Joseph never would have let Mary and her little baby lie there in a dirty crib. Even they knew that Jesus would not inhabit any place that is not clean.

Some people would rather have the dirt than the Son of God. They would rather live in darkness than come to the light. "And this is the condemnation, that light is come into the world, and men loved darkness rather than light, because their deeds were evil" (John 3:19).

This is the reason people today do not receive Him. They have the Bible, a hymnbook, churches, radio preachers and evangelists. They have opportunities; they have light; they have information; but they will not receive Him, because if they do, they are going to have to clean up. Some people will not clean up. They do not want their houses to be clean. They love their dirt.

A Change in Direction

A fourth reason they would not accept Jesus was that it would mean a complete change in direction for them. It would have meant a thorough housecleaning inside of them and an aggregation of self. He said, "Let him take up his cross and follow me."

As strange as it may seem, many would choose sin over Jesus; they would rather have buzzards perch in their hearts than the heavenly dove come in. As long as the buzzards are there, the dove will never descend. As long as the world's dirt remains in the heart, Jesus Christ will never come in. "He came unto His own and His own people would not receive Him because they loved dirt." People love inward moral dirt. They may look respectable and wear fashionable clothes and sure-shined shoes, drive the latest and newest automobile, have a modern kitchen and bathroom and live by push buttons; but inside the heart there is a filthy pool. Jesus Christ will not come in until you drain it all.

"He came unto His own people and His own people received Him not." Nothing is different today. When the Lord says, "All right, I'll help you and get rid of this mess," we say, "No, Jesus, I love that mess. I was brought up in it. I want to be respectable and I want to be outwardly clean and I want the sepulchre of my life to be carefully polished and painted, but I do not want to get rid of the dead men's bones inside. I love those dead men's bones, and I don't want to get rid of them."

Some clean, respectable, well-groomed people will leave church on a Sunday morning and take dead men's bones out with them in the sanctuary of their soul. They will not let Jesus Christ come in and cleanse the temple. They would rather have the slime there.

"Let him take up his cross and follow me"—we do not want to do that. Few want to be that serious.

Risking Wholehearted Trust

The reason they rejected Christ was that it would have meant faith in the unseen. They would have had to throw themselves on

God. They would have to give up their tangible comforts and trust completely in Jesus Christ.

Before we get too self-righteous in accusing those Jews that received Him not 2,000 years ago, let us not forget that nothing has changed. In pointing to them we take the spotlight off of ourselves. It eases our conscience little to remind ourselves that it was the Jews that received Him not. But I warn against any such self-deception as that.

After 2,000 years of tradition behind us that the Jews did not have, we, more than anybody else, should be embracing, accepting and receiving Jesus Christ. We have revelation that the Jews did not have. They had the Old Testament. We have the Old Testament and the New. We have information the Old Testament Jew did not have. We have light they did not have. We have opportunities they did not have, and we have an urgency through the presence of the Holy Ghost that they did not have. I do not think for one minute that we ought to spend our time belaboring the Jew and comforting our own carnal hearts by saying, "He came to His own world and the Jews did not receive Him." We would only be building the sepulchres of our fathers, as Jesus said, and we would be as bad as they that slew the prophets. We had better look to our own hearts.

We Love Our Sin More

Here we have the "Light of the world," the very Son of God, and we cannot get up enough steam or enthusiasm even to keep from looking bored when we talk about Him.

I wonder if we have been converted at all. Nobody can understand Christianity until they are in it. We cannot stand back and look on to understand we must be converted over into it by a miracle, and then we can understand Christianity. Then we can understand God and Christ. But until Jesus Christ is received—the miracle-working, transforming power into the light—there never can be any salvation or any understanding of the things of God.

All nature received Him. The very brown cutworm that crawls across the road fulfills His word. "Praise Him all ye stars of light," says the Holy Ghost. "Praise ye Him trees, forests, hills and mountains," says the Holy Ghost. "The beast of the field shall glorify Me," says the Holy Ghost. And all nature sings to meet their Lord. A little hard, selfish, sinful man rejects the Son of God.

I believe this to be more terrible than atom bombs, more terrible than wars to the death and more terrible than diseases. What shall we answer Him when the very nature He created receives Him and our hard hearts say, "I want my money, I want that girl, I want that fame, I want that job, I want that pleasure. I want, I want." Always "I want." That the Son of God stands outside of this is the tragedy of humanity.

If some Shakespeare could write the vast, elemental, boundless, fathomless tragedy of humanity, it would be that we loved our sin more than we loved our God. The world around us sang when He came and will sing again when He comes in glory, but our hard hearts say no. The tragedy is that we have rejected Him from our hearts because we want our own way. We will have our own way when Jesus Christ shall park on the sidewalk outside. The stars will sympathize and the birds, the worms, the cat, but we will let Him stand on the outside.

We ought to be ashamed of ourselves, and we ought to open the door of our heart and let Him in. "He came unto His own world and it received Him but He came unto His own people and they rejected Him." How terrible. This is the tragic side of Christ's coming into His world.

5

THE MYSTERY OF THE WORD MADE FLESH

And the Word was made flesh, and dwelt among us, (and we beheld his glory, the glory as of the only begotten of the Father,) full of grace and truth.
JOHN 1:14

The word "mystery" is often used carelessly and, consequently, has been misused. There is mystery in the sense of a Sherlock Holmes mystery. Simply collect all of the clues and you can solve the mystery. But when the word "mystery" is used in the sense that I have used it in relation to Christ, it has to do with that aspect of Christ that can never be discovered. The apostle John attempts to lift us into the mystery of God and into the circles of deity far beyond the pursuit of man. Realms so high, lofty and noble that it is impossible to us to follow to its conclusion. All I can hope to do is gaze heavenward in wonder and long after the mystery of God.

The phrase that stirs up the sense of mystery is, "And the Word was made flesh" (John 1:14). In six simple words, the apostle states the most profound mystery of human thought—how deity could cross the gulf separating what is God from what is not God. Although man in all of his scientific advancement has made the world very complex, John the apostle breaks down the entire universe into two things: God and not God. To explain this mystery in as simple words as possible, let me say that the universe is made up of that which is God and that which is not God, and all that which is not God was made by God, but God was made by none. The mystery is compounded by the fact that between that which is God and that which is not God is a great and impassable gulf.

The most profound mystery of human flaw is how the creator could join Himself to the creature. How the "Word," meaning Christ, could be made "flesh," meaning the creature, is one of the most amazing mysteries to contemplate. Some may not think it is so amazing, but those who have meditated on this will be amazed at the unbridgeable gulf between God and not God. A gulf is fixed, a vast gulf of infinitude, and how God managed to bridge that gulf and join Himself to His creatures and limit the limitless is beyond our comprehension. In the language we hear more properly, how can the infinite ever become the finite, and how can that which has no limit deliberately impose upon Himself limitations?

It is the arrogance of man that believes that he is, or at least acts as though he is, the only order of being. The Bible clearly teaches that humanity is only one order of God's creation. There are angels and cherubim and seraphim and creatures and watchers and holy ones and all of these strange principalities and powers that walk so darkly and brightly through the passages of the Bible. In light of this, why would God favor one above the other? In the book of Hebrews, we read, "For verily he took not on him the nature of angels; but he took on him the seed of Abraham" (Heb. 2:16).

Were we doing it, knowing humanity as we do, we might have been tempted to select the order of angels or seraphim, supposing that it would not be quite as much a step down as it would be with man. Abraham certainly was not equal to an angel. The mystery of it all is, He came down to the lowest order and took upon Himself the nature and seed of Abraham. Even Paul, who is declared one of the six greatest intellects of all time, threw up his hands and said, "Great is the mystery of godliness" (1 Tim. 3:16).

I often think of the wise words of John Wesley: "Distinguish the act from the method by which the act is performed and do not reject the fact because you do not know how it was done." In coming to the mystery of that which is Christ incarnate, we reverently bow our heads and confess, "It is so, God, but we don't know how." I will not reject the fact because I do not know the operation by which it was brought to pass.

The Incarnation of Christ is shrouded in impenetrable mystery that we could never uncover with our finite thinking. But there is one thing that we can know for sure: The Incarnation required no compromise of deity. When the "Word was made flesh," His deity did not suffer. Before His Incarnation, Christ was absolute deity; after His Incarnation, He was just as much deity as before. His deity suffered nothing when He became flesh. This mystery baffles us when we meditate upon the person of Christ.

The old Greek and Roman world was full of gods that were compromisers one way or another. But the holy God who is God, and all else is not God, that God who is "our Father who art in heaven," would never compromise Himself. This mystery of the Incarnation was accomplished without any compromise of the deity. God did not degrade Himself by this condescension. He did not in any sense make Himself to be less than God. He remained God, and everything else remained not God; the gulf still existed, even after Jesus Christ had become man and had dwelt among us. So instead of God degrading Himself when He became man, He, by the act of Incarnation, elevated mankind to Himself.

God and Man Together

Personally, I like to think about those early ages of man. I read and meditate on those first chapters of Genesis with great interest. The thing that really charms my soul is the communion God enjoyed with Adam and Eve in the Garden. I am sure it went both ways. I read with great fascination that God came and walked in the Garden in the cool of the day, fellowshipping with Adam and Eve. That fellowship was customary for them, because God made man in His image and did not degrade Himself by communing with man.

As wonderful as that fellowship was, it was only temporary. "In the cool of the day," the Scripture tells us, God was able to dwell with man; then something interrupted that marvelous fellowship.

In the beginning, God dwelt with man. That fellowship was wonderful, but Adam and Eve sinned, forcing God to drive them out of that garden setting, away from His presence. Following that, God never dwelt with man in quite the same way. Occasionally, He would appear in what theologians call a theophany, an appearance of the deity. But He dwelt in the Shekinah, hidden in the fire and the cloud.

We have many examples of God walking with man. But this was intermittent and temporary compared to what it was prior to the Fall.

Take for example, Enoch. The Bible says, "And Enoch walked with God: and he was not; for God took him" (Gen. 5:24). I can just imagine the fellowship those two had together. Then one day the walk took longer than usual and God looked at Enoch and said, "My house is closer. Why don't you come home with Me tonight?" And Enoch just disappeared.

Then there was Abraham, called the friend of God. "And the scripture was fulfilled which saith, Abraham believed God, and it was imputed unto him for righteousness: and he was called the Friend of God" (Jas. 2:23). I do not know any title I would prefer than "The Friend of God." Just thinking about this causes cravings and desires in my heart toward God. What wonderful fellowship these two "friends" had together.

The Old Testament is filled with such examples, but these encounters were brief and for the most part veiled—when God showed Himself to Moses in the fire of the bush or while Moses was hidden in the cleft of the rock. God only allowed the trailing parts of His garments to be seen. The eyes of men were not able to look upon the majesty of the deity.

God, who once dwelt only intermittently with men, suddenly came and "the word was made flesh and dwelt amongst us." He now dwelt with men in person, and they called His name Emmanuel, which means "God with us."

I want you to take note of three prepositions here. Notice when He appeared as man, He appeared to dwell *with* men in person and to be united *to* men, then ultimately to dwell *in* men forever. So it is "with men" and "to men" and "in men" that He came to dwell.

The Glory of the Son

The apostle John said, "We beheld," or "they beheld." What was it that he is calling attention to? It is simply the glory of the Son. But what was that glory? When we look at the Son what is the glory that shines forth?

Is it the glory of His works? All of the Gospels depict the mighty works and miracles that Jesus performed. From that first miracle of turning the water into wine to the very last, Jesus was a wonderworker. His works included feeding the 5,000, healing the sick, raising the dead, walking on water, casting out demons. All of these were dramatic miracles.

I am reminded of a grand hymn often sung in the church, "The Love of God," written by Frederick M. Lehman (1868–1953):

Could we with ink the ocean fill,
And were the skies of parchment made,
Were every stalk on earth a quill,
And every man a scribe by trade,
To write the love of God above
Would drain the ocean dry.
Nor could the scroll contain the whole,
Though stretched from sky to sky.

Toward the end of his Gospel, John writes, "And many other signs truly did Jesus in the presence of his disciples, which are not written in this book" (John 20:30). Even John could not keep track of all the wonders and miracles that Jesus did. Everything our Lord did while walking among them was wonderful. But is this the glory that John speaks of? Is this what captured his attention and admiration?

Throughout Jesus' ministry, whatever He did was wonderful. How tender, how kind when the woman who was bleeding for more than 12 years received a sudden deliverance, and with a sudden word He staunched the debilitating flow of blood. She went away with a shining face to tell everybody that the hem of His garment had healing power in it. So the works of our Lord were always dramatic and amazing.

We Beheld His Glory

Often you will hear sermons on the radio making physical healing of the body and works of the miraculous everything. I wish that I could go along with such interpretation and say the glory of Jesus Christ lay in His ability to cast out devils, to heal the sick and raise the dead and still the waves. Undoubtedly, that was wonderful, and He did get some praise to Himself from those necessary acts of miracles, but I believe there was a greater glory than merely works of wonder, which our Lord manifested.

It must always be kept in mind that what God thinks about a man is more important than what a man thinks about himself. As far as God is concerned, what a man is always is more important to God than what that man does. We judge a man by his performance, by what he can contribute. But God sees deeper inside and bores to the very core of what that man really is. God is look-ing for goodness. It is his character and personality that God looks for. God is never impressed by anything a man can do.

Now bring this over to Christ. What was it that made Him glorious? It was what Jesus was that made Him the glorious person that John writes about. His glory lay in the fact that He was perfect in a loveless world; He was purity in an impure world; He was meekness in a harsh and quarrelsome world. Everything that the world was, Christ was the exact opposite. That was what made Him glorious. "We beheld his glory" re-ferred to the deathless devotion of Christ and His patient suf-fering and unquenchable life, and the grace and truth at work in Him. He was the glory of the only begotten Son from the Father, full of grace and truth. That was what made Jesus won-derful. That was His glory among men.

All of this is little known in the world today. Men and women in all their wild, money-inspired and profit-inspired revelries are not celebrating the great miracle of turning the wa-ter into wine. Neither are they celebrating all of the healing acts that Jesus did: the raising of the dead, the cursing of a fig tree, or any of the other miracles that Jesus Christ did (see Mark 11:12-14,20-21; Luke 22:49-51).

The poor world around us, lost in the depravity of its own heart, with little remnants of religious instinct left, does not celebrate what Jesus was. The glory of the Son was that He was God walking among men. Here was something that was not man, but yet was man. Here was God among men. Here was a man acting like God in the midst of sinful men, and this was the wonder of it all.

Being in the Very Form of God . . .

We celebrate a man today who was God made flesh. We celebrate the deep, dark mystery of the miracle of that which was not God being taken up into God, and being made flesh, so that we now have Jesus Christ who is God and yet who is man. Out of His fullness, we receive. Does it mean that everybody has received the fullness of Jesus Christ? No, it cannot mean that.

What does it mean? Simply that Jesus Christ, the eternal Son, is the only medium in which God dispenses His benefits to His creation. Only through Christ will God dispense blessings on humanity. It is Christ the eternal Son through whom God dispenses His benefits to His creation.

Because Jesus is the eternal Son, because He is of the eternal generation and equal with the Father as pertaining to His substance, His eternity, His love, His power, His grace, His goodness and all the other attributes of deity, He is the channel. He is the medium through which God dispenses all His blessings, all His fullness of all that we receive, as the doe that goes down to the edge of the lake and drinks. Have you received the fullness of the lake? The doe might answer, "Yes and no. I am full from the lake, but I have not received of the fullness of the lake. I did not drink the lake down; I drank what I can hold of the lake."

Grace upon Grace

Out of His fullness, God has given us through Jesus Christ grace upon grace, so that the only medium through which God does anything is His Son. Whether He created or whether He is creating, it is all through Jesus Christ our Lord. If He speaks, it is through the eternal Word. If He reveals Himself, it is because

He who was in the bosom of the Father has revealed Him. If He provides, it is through the medium of Jesus Christ. If He sustains it, it is because it can be said, "He is before all things, and by him all things consist" (Col. 1:17).

Wherever the voice of the creature crosses the vast gulf to the ears of the Creator, grace must operate. We have restricted grace to John 3:16. We must have forgotten that everything God does is out of the grace of His fullness. The only thing that can cross that vast gulf is that amazing grace of God. The great hymn writer, John Newton, put all of this into lyric beauty in his hymn "Amazing Grace":

Amazing Grace, how sweet the sound,
That saved a wretch like me. . . .
I once was lost but now am found,
Was blind, but now, I see.

As amazing as this hymn is, it is just the beginning. John Newton goes on to say:

Through many dangers, toils, and snares
I have already come.
'Tis Grace hath brought me safe thus far,
And Grace will lead me home.

Whatever any creature has, the amazing grace of God is channeled from God to that creature. It is grace upon grace.

Even before a person has put his faith and trust in Jesus Christ he is a recipient of God's grace. Even the person who refuses Christ cannot get away from the channel of blessing flowing into his heart and life. He may spend all of eternity in the hell prepared for the devil and his demons, but while he is upon earth, he is a recipient of grace upon grace. Everything God does is by grace. No man, no creature, deserves anything. Salvation is by grace alone. All that God does flows out of grace.

Without exception, everyone has received grace from God. Everyone has received life and a mind that stores up memories of a lifetime. All of that is evidence of God's grace toward humanity.

The whole universe is God's beneficiary and joins to give praise to the Lamb that was slain. Under the earth, on the earth, and above the earth, John heard creatures praising Jesus Christ, and all joined, "Saying with a loud voice, Worthy is the Lamb that was slain to receive power, and riches, and wisdom, and strength, and honour, and glory, and blessing" (Rev. 5:12).

"Thou art worthy, O Lord, to receive glory and honour and power: for thou hast created all things, and for thy pleasure they are and were created" (Rev. 4:11) tells us that the whole universe is a beneficiary of Jesus Christ.

Jesus Christ Is All in All

This is where our witnessing to the non-Christians is important. Everybody we witness to has already benefited from Christ. In our witnessing, we are simply presenting Christ in His new office. Apart from the Lord Jesus Christ, God never did anything. Throughout all of His universe, God works through the Son.

When we go to an unsaved person and say, "Believe on the Lord Jesus Christ," we are only saying, believe on the One who sustains you and upholds you and has given you life and pities you and spares you and keeps you. Believe on the One out of whom you came. All of His fullness we have received, or we have received out of His fullness, and we only present Jesus as Lord and Savior.

There are those who would offer a divided Christ. They say, in effect, "Accept Christ now as your Savior." And then later on say, "Now, accept Christ as your Lord." The Bible does not teach anything of the sort.

There is no Saviorhood without Lordship. Jesus Christ is both Lord and Savior, and He was Lord before He was Savior; and if He's not Lord, He's not Savior. When we present this Eternal Word that was made flesh and dwelt among us to men as Lord and Savior, we present Him only in His other offices. Previously He has been Creator, Sustainer and Benefactor. Now we ask men to believe on Him as Lord and Savior; but it is the same Lord Jesus.

The suggestion that the Old Testament is a book of law and the New Testament a book of grace is a false premise. There is as much grace and mercy and love in the Old Testament as there is in the New. There is more about hell in the New Testament than there is in the Old. When it comes to judgment and the fury of God burning with fire upon simple men and simple creatures, it is found in the New Testament, not in the Old. If you want excoriation, blisters and burns, do not go to Jeremiah, go to Jesus Christ.

The God of the Old Testament is the God of the New, and the Father of the Old Testament is the Father of the New Testament. The Christ who was made flesh to dwell among us is the Christ who walked through all the pages of the Old Testament. Was it the law that forgave David when he committed his immoral sin? No, it was grace. Was it grace that said, "Babylon has fallen, the great harlot is fallen, Babylon, is fallen"? No, it was law.

There is perfect and absolute harmony between all persons of the Godhead. What he says here is the contrast between all that Moses could do and all that Christ could do. Moses gave the law. That was all Moses could do, for he was not the channel through which God dispensed grace. God chose His only begotten Son.

Here lies the contrast: "the law was given by Moses, but grace and truth came by Jesus Christ," means only that all that Moses could do was command righteousness; but Jesus Christ produces righteousness. All that Moses could do was forbid us to sin; but Jesus Christ came to save us from sin. This is not to pit one against the other, but to show one doing what the other could not do. For Moses could not save, but Jesus could. The Holy Ghost, in Romans 10:4-7, said the law Moses gave was holy, just and good and must not be spoken against. But it could not save. But because Jesus Christ is the eternal Son, the channel through which God dispenses grace to the world, grace came through Jesus Christ.

Grace precedes everything—from the first day of creation until the Virgin Mary gave birth in a Bethlehem manger. For it was the grace of God in Christ that saved the human race from extinction when they sinned in the Garden. It was the grace of God in Jesus Christ yet to be born that saved the eighth person when the Flood covered the earth. And it was the grace of God in Jesus Christ yet to be born, but existing in preincarnation glory, that forgave David when he committed his sin; that forgave Abraham when he lied; that enabled Abraham to pray God down to 10 righteous persons when He was threatening to destroy Sodom; that forgave Israel repeatedly.

It was the grace of God in Christ yet before the Incarnation that made God say, "I have risen early in the morning and stretched out My hands unto you." It made him say, "Like as a father pitieth his children, so the LORD pitieth them that fear him" (Ps. 103:13). Jesus is the channel through which grace comes. And He said, "I am the truth," and it is through Him that grace is released to the world, through His wounded side, to sinners like you and me. All the grace of God anywhere comes through Jesus Christ. Then he says, "No man hath seen God at any time; the only begotten Son, which is in the bosom of the Father, he hath declared him" (John 1:18).

The Mystery of the Sacrificial Atonement

All through His ministry, Jesus was God acting like God. He deliberately crossed the mysterious gulf between God and not God. He took upon Him the form of a man to become flesh, and dwelt among us. Notice, it is not who *was in* the bosom or who *will be* in the bosom, but always *who is* in the bosom. It is the language of continuous being. Even while hanging on the cross, Christ did not leave the bosom of the Father.

How then could He cry, "My God, my God, why hast thou forsaken me" (Matt. 27:46)? Was He frightened, was He mistaken? Never. He was never mistaken about anything. Then what was it? The answer is very plain. Even when Christ died on the cross for humanity, He never divided the godhead. You cannot divide the substance. Not all the swords of Nero could ever cut through the substance of the godhead, could ever cut off the Father from the Son.

It was the man who cried, "Why hast thou forsaken me?" It was Mary's son who cried. It was the body God gave Him. It was the Lamb about to die. It was the sacrifice that cried. It was the human Jesus; it was the Son of man that cried. But the ancient and timeless deity was never separated. And He was still in the bosom of the Father when He cried, "Father, into thy hands I commend my spirit: and having said thus, he gave up the ghost" (Luke 23:46). For Father, Son and Holy Ghost are forever one—inseparable, indivisible—and can never be anything else.

The eternal Father never turned His back on the eternal Word, for He was always in the bosom of the Father. But the eternal Father turned His back upon the Son—the Son of man, the sacrifice of the Lamb to be slain—and in the blind terror and pain of it all, the sacrifice, the Lamb, temporarily became sin for us and knew Himself forsaken. And God dumped all that vast bubbling, boiling, seething, dirty, slimy mess of human sin on the soul of His Son and then backed away. And in that moment of anguish, the Son cried, "Why have you forsaken me?" But in the next breath, He could say, "Father, into thy hands I commend my spirit." The cross did not divide the godhead. Nothing could ever do that. One forever, indivisible, the substance undivided, the persons unconfounded.

The mystery of atonement had to be performed. Why in the Old Testament did the priests go behind the veil? To perform the ritual of atonement and then come out from behind the veil; and priests specially prepared rushed to close that thick veil and hide the Holy Place. It was God saying in beautiful symbolism that there would be a day when another Priest with other blood should enter into a realm where the mind of man could never penetrate. There, in the mystery too deep and dark and wonderful for man to understand, all alone, with none to help Him. Not David, not Abraham, not Paul—no one.

God stepped back and allowed Him to die, and briefly and quickly His heart was joined again to the love of God. Three days later, He was raised from the dead and ascended to the right hand of God the Father Almighty, when He should come to judge the quick and the dead (see 2 Tim. 4:1).

He Has Shown Us the Father

Now the closing line, "He hath declared him" (John 1:18). What has He declared about God? There are profundities that He could never declare; there are depths that He could never declare; but there are some things that He could declare and did declare and does declare. He declared God's holy being and, above all, for us poor sinners, He declared His love and His mercy. So He set God forth, and Jesus Christ tells us in His tender human being that God has a care for us.

I think of how easy it might have been for God to keep silent. In fact, there are many who feel that God is doing just that now. I shudder to think of His silent voice, the incommunicable heart of God, His mind inexpressible. This is not the true picture of God, for God is always speaking. His voice rises above the din and clatter of the world around us.

I love the story of Elijah. A marvelous, wonderful man of God he was before a tremendously pagan world. Due to some dire circumstances, Elijah finds himself hiding in a cave. It is in the cave that Elijah hears the voice of God. "And after the earthquake a fire; but the LORD was not in the fire: and after the fire a still small voice" (1 Kings 19:12).

It is not that God is not speaking or communicating to us. Rather, we have allowed ourselves to get back into such a hole that all we hear is the noise around us. Only after all of that noise has spent itself do we begin to hear in the silence of our heart that still, small, most mighty voice of God speaking to us.

God loves us and cares for us. God has a plan for us and is in fact carrying out that way. Jesus has set forth God before us. He revealed God's grace, mercy, good and redemptive intention. He set forth, brought it and gave it to us. Now we have only to turn and believe and accept and take and follow. And it is ours.

Thank God for the Truth, for the Word, for the eternal Son, for the One we present to you as Lord and Savior.

6

THE OLD TESTAMENT MESSIAH VERSUS THE NEW TESTAMENT CHRIST

The next day John seeth Jesus coming unto him, and saith,
Behold the Lamb of God, which taketh away the sin of the world.
This is he of whom I said, After me cometh a man which is
preferred before me: for he was before me.

JOHN 1:29-37

One of the most beautiful things I know of in the Scriptures is how John, with all of Palestine listening to him, arrived at a moment in his life when he said, "My work is finished and the one that I came before has arrived; I must decrease and He must increase. I fade out, and now He shines in His splendor."

John was about to pass out of the picture to shine no more, and he had told them many things about the coming one. He had not seen the coming one yet. It is a mistake to believe that John and Jesus were acquainted with each other, even though they were distant relatives. Or if they were acquainted with each other, John had no remote conception that Jesus was to be the One he was preaching about. John had told them many things about the coming One, and now he crowns all that he has to say by saying, "Behold the Lamb of God, which taketh away the sin of the world" (John 1:29).

What did that mean to a Jew? You would have to be a Jew with a background of understanding in the Jewish religion to be able to have this hit your heart with the brilliant sunburst that came to them when John the Baptist said, "Behold the Lamb of God."

They knew the story of Abel, the young man who had taken the lamb and brought its dripping blood to the altar of God, and the fire of God had fallen, and God witnessed to Abel that he was accepted. They knew the story of Abraham making his sacrifice. They were perfectly familiar with that wonderful Passover lamb slain for the salvation of a race. And they were familiar with that long line of priests that had offered lambs year after year down to that time; and when John said, "Behold the Lamb of God," it was like saying, "Now that we're at the bottom of the column, we'll add it up. All the lambs that ever have been, from Abel's first lamb down to this hour, all receive their fulfillment in the Lamb of God.

The lamb of Abel and the lamb of Abraham and the lamb of Isaac and the lamb of Judah and the Passover lamb, all these were in the lambs that men had presented. But now comes the lamb that nobody else could ever present. He is God Almighty's Lamb, the summation and finish of all the lambs that ever were or are to be. This is the full, clean preliminary summation of what all the dying lambs meant through the centuries. And that must have come to the ears of the Jews with wonderful meaning. "Behold the Lamb of God, which taketh away the sin of the world" (John 1:29).

John the Baptist testifies, "This was he of whom I spake, He that cometh after me is preferred before me: for he was before me" (v. 15). In this passage, there is a little antithetical trick of language that must be broken down. "He that cometh after me," in time, who is "preferred before me," in honor, because He was before me in rank. "There cometh one after me," that is, "I came first, and I came as the herald proclaiming the one who is to come after me; but the one who came after me in time is preferred before me in honor, because He is before me in rank in that He is the very Son of God Himself."

Of course, the big problem was how this one was to be identified. Great multitudes of people were being baptized, so how was this coming One to be recognized? To prove He was the Messiah, He had to meet certain rigid tests. He had to be born of the seed of Abraham. Nobody could claim to be the Son of God or claim to be the Savior of humanity—Israel's Messiah—and not be of the seed of Abraham. He had to be able to trace His lineage back to Abraham. That had to be; otherwise, if they could not prove He was not the Christ, He could not prove He was.

It was narrowed down still further. He had to be born of the seed of Isaac and Jacob. Jacob had 12 sons, and the Messiah would have to come through one man, David. Not only must He be born of the lineage of Abraham through David the king, but He also must be born at an approximate time. If He had been born 300 years before, as Buddha was, it would not have done. If He had been born 600 years after, as Mohammed was, it would not have been sufficient. If He had been born an Arab or Japanese, it would not have done, because He would have missed the lineage element.

Then, He must be born in a certain country. It was not an important country as the world saw it—just a little country tucked up there somewhat pushed in between the continents. But if He were born anywhere else, Rome or Egypt or India, that would not have done. He had to be born in that little country.

Not only did He have to be born in that particular country, but His birthplace also had to be pinpointed to an actual place, a little tiny town that did not have more than one inn. The Scriptures are very specific, and they say that there was no room for Him in the inn. You do not go to New York or Chicago and say there was no room for Him in the hotel. You might be able to say, "I couldn't get a room in any hotel."

But in little Bethlehem of Judah, it was said there was no room for Him in the inn. There was only one inn, and they rarely used that. But it so happened they needed to use it at that time because of a decree that had gone out from Caesar Augustus. So He had to be born in that little town.

If you and I had been in charge of the birth of the Messiah, we would have had Him born in Rome, because Rome was the eternal city. We would have Him born in Athens, certainly, because that was the city of brains. We would have picked a city somewhere big enough and important enough to thrust itself into the human consciousness.

God works silently, quietly and modestly and is turning a world over, for He does it so quietly that no one notices. He had

His Messiah born in little Bethlehem of Judah. Judah's little cities were not very large, only Jerusalem could be considered a large city. "But thou, Bethlehem Ephratah, though thou be little among the thousands of Judah, yet out of thee shall he come forth unto me that is to be ruler in Israel; whose goings forth have been from of old, from everlasting" (Mic. 5:2).

John the Baptist knew all of this but it still was not enough. Many men born of the seed of Abraham were living at that time. Men who were the descendants of the Lion of David were living at that time. I do not know if there were any that were born at Bethlehem, but there might have been.

When Jesus presented Himself at the bank of the Jordan, there was something different about the man, but not enough difference. John looked at Him, felt inferior and said, "I don't feel right about baptizing you, whoever you are. I think you ought to baptize me." He still did not know who it was, and our Lord said, "For thus it becometh us to fulfill all righteousness" (Matt. 3:15).

When John baptized Jesus, the Holy Ghost descended, and John said, "And I knew him not: but he that sent me to baptize with water, the same said unto me, Upon whom thou shalt see the Spirit descending, and remaining on him, the same is he which baptizeth with the Holy Ghost" (John 1:33).

So Jesus met all those rigid tests.

Messianic Prophecies Fulfilled

One evangelical very much influenced by liberal theology said, "I believe a Messianic thread runs through the Old Testament alright, and I believe that there is a Messianic hope in the Old

Testament, but I do not believe that the Old Testament ever prophesied about Jesus Christ. Christians have read back in through the Old Testament what they know about Jesus and made it add up to Jesus Christ our Lord."

Comments like this make me spiritually indignant. I do not ask for any patronizing concessions from liberal theologians. They do not owe me anything. And I believe, and am perfectly willing, that my faith in God and Christ and all my hope for the world to come and all of Christendom should rest upon the simple fact that the Jesus of the New Testament is the Messiah of the Old. I do not want to be patronized, and I do not want to be as they cruelly say, "I understand you."

I do not want them understanding me. They owe me nothing, and I make no concessions that Jesus of the New Testament is the Messiah of the Old. They cannot fool me by insisting it is just general prophecies that do not mean anything in particular. If I believed that, I would slam my Bible shut; I would give it one goodbye and never insult a congregation again by preaching to them. But the Jesus of the New Testament is the Messiah prophesied in the Old, and I will not allow anyone to frighten me out of that.

We can prove our position by the Scriptures; and if any man would admit the authority of the Word of God, we can show how the Jesus of the New Testament came according to the Old Testament Scriptures and walked in all the ways pointed out for Him thousands of years before He was born. He appeared at a certain time, in a certain place and moved with the fine precision of the most expensive watch. Everything happened as God Almighty in the Old Testament prophesied.

I do not know why that is so hard to believe. Why should it seem incredible that God Almighty should be able to foretell the future? God has lived all our tomorrows and knows no yesterday and no tomorrow but swallows up yesterday and tomorrow in one everlasting now. It would be easy for God to know what would take place in our tomorrow when He has already lived it and looks back upon all our tomorrows as something already accomplished.

Let me pose a few questions to those who patronize the Scriptures and insist that the Bible is a general book and it is not specific. The Bible is just as specific as a doctor is. A man feels ill and when he goes to a doctor, the doctor does not reach under the table and pull out a general book of symptoms and say, "I'm not going to prescribe specifically now. I'm just going to give you a general prescription."

What kind of crazy business would that be? I would not want any medicine prescribed generally. I want to know the prescription is for me and not somebody else. A pill that would cure somebody else could kill me. When you come to anything as fine as prescribing for the human body, you have to be specific about the medicine or someone might die.

God, in His infinite wisdom, is specific in all things. Many would just accuse us of being uneducated. I have talked to some supposed to be so well educated but when it comes to the Bible they are functionally illiterate. These theological liberals talk about William Wordsworth and Søren Kierkegaard and get poetical and dreamy-eyed and stretch their arms out to embrace all men as brothers. But not one of them can say, "I have seen Him, I have known Him and He walks along with me." Not a one.

I do not think I will turn liberal, not at this stage. They have nothing that interests me. I am satisfied with the Book. I am satisfied with the holy Book that prophesied the coming of that holy thing which was born of Mary.

When John the Baptist saw Him, he had all the proof he needed and said, "Behold the Lamb of God." The trouble with the world is not hard to diagnose. John the Baptist correctly diagnosed the trouble when he said, "Behold the Lamb of God, which taketh away the sin of the world" (John 1:29). He emphatically pointed out that there is only one hope for the burdened heart of the world, only one. There is only one hope for the salvation of the world.

What is to prevent the human race from destroying itself? Those words and thoughts are in the hearts of men, and they are wondering about the human race destroying itself. What is to prevent some insane dictator from bringing the world down around him?

The A-bomb has given way to the H-bomb, and there is another bomb more terribly deadly than the H-bomb. The Cobalt bomb is still more terrible than that H-bomb. What is to prevent some mad dictator from saying, "I'll rule the world or ruin it"? He will rule it or bring it down into ruins around his own suicidal head.

What is to prevent some huge accident from taking place? What is to prevent someone setting up some vast unstoppable chain reaction that will burn up the world? I will tell you what will prevent it. God Almighty has not given the world up. Philosophers may have, but God has not. God is not finished with the world.

A Restored World

When I gaze into the future, I am optimistic. Even if some country like Russia should conquer the world, I would still be optimistic as long as they let me live. I would go to heaven optimistic when they made me die. I do not believe God has given up His world. I believe the human race was created in the image of God and though we fell into shameful disgrace and moral tragedy, God Almighty sent Someone to restore us again to that holy place from which we fell. I believe in the ultimate restoration of the world.

Let me explain what I mean. I believe that the control of the world is going to pass from that unregenerate part of the world into the hands of the regenerate, for there are now two human races. There was once one human race, and that human race fell and plunged down into the mire of sin and iniquity, and brought about disease, insanity and death.

God began the redemption of the human race within the race so that there are now two races running parallel to each other. The unregenerate race that goes back to the loins of Adam and the regenerate race that goes back to the start of Jesus. The firstborn man and the second-born man; the once-born man and the twice-born man; the son of Adam and the Son of God. They are mingled together in the world now, and for the time being, the race is in the hands of the unregenerate world. The world is ruled by unregenerate statesmen, presidents, prime ministers, leaders, kings and generals. And if there is not help from some other direction, these unregenerate worldlings are going to bring our world down in ruins by some Cobalt bomb or some other hellish thing dreamed up from the pit.

But there is another race, "a chosen generation, a royal priest-hood, an holy nation, a peculiar people; that ye should shew forth the praises of him who hath called you out of darkness into his marvellous light" (1 Pet. 2:9). As God took Eve out of the side of Adam and formed a woman, so out of the wounded heart of Jesus, God is forming a new race, and that new race is going to be the ultimate human race. And this fallen, lost race is going to be sent out from God into the far places, like the scapegoat, to bear their sins into the ultimate hell that God has prepared for the devil and his angels. But the new human race, which you are a part of by the new birth, will finally take over the world.

Was this only a poetic dream when Jesus said, "Blessed are the meek: for they shall inherit the earth"? Was that only one more religious cliché, one more bromide to give a little bit of false hope to the world? No, "Blessed are the meek: for they shall inherit the earth" (Matt. 5:5) and some wit thought that he would get himself up a little joke so he said, "Yes, blessed are the meek for they shall inherit the earth after the proud are through with it." He was telling more truth than he knew. They will be through with it all right, when they are thrown out of it. And all that rests on guns and bombs, and cheap politics, on human sci-ence, on human society will be swept away and God will plant a new race in the earth with Jesus Christ the King.

Every sinner belongs to the old race. Every newborn Chris-tian belongs to the new race. There are only two kinds of peo-ple in the world: those whose essential life stems from the loins of Adam, and those whose essential life stems from the heart of Jesus. So the church of God on earth is simply a sample of the new race; that is all.

If we are a redeemed people and samples of the new race, we ought to live like the new race and think like the new race and act like the new race of people. Not only the individual but also ultimately the sin of society will purge this world and make it clean, and will rule.

The Lamb that Was Slain

Last, and best of all for you and me, is that He "taketh away the sin of the world" (John 1:29). If we come to Him with our sins— just come to Him as we are—He does it.

While living in the state of West Virginia, there was a middle-aged woman in our congregation. I have never known anybody like her before or since. She was so gloomy that her attitude could almost sour milk. She was the epitome of all things pessimistic, gloomy and blue. The world had ended for her. She would come down to our house and visit, and we would pray with her.

Seeing her coming down the street was an experience. I cannot describe her other than to say that she was misery personified, but, thank God, she was praying. Then one morning, the door opened and she burst through; only instead of crepe hanging on the moon, it was now the sun newly risen. She burst in full of sunshine and delight and joy and said, "He's done it, He's done it, the Lord has done it, He's done it." She was almost hysterical with laughter, delight and joy. I knew her for a long time after that, and she never lost it. This "Lamb of God, which taketh away the sin of the world" had suddenly found that poor sin-cursed heart of hers and set her bells to ringing.

Suppose that the politicians decided to give a tax reduction. Word comes down from Washington D.C., saying, "We're going to reduce taxes 20 percent." It is not specific, just general, and does not mean anybody in particular. I think I would wire Washington and say, "Does that mean me?" Suppose a lawyer called you in and said so-and-so died and left a million dollars, but it is just general, not for anybody. That information is not important to you personally and does not affect you. And we're supposed to believe that represents superior thinking and scholarship. The Lamb of God came for a specific reason and for precise people that He could bless through His redeeming grace. This is given to us by definite promises of the Word of God.

Thousands of simple-hearted people once bound by liquor can say today, "The Lamb of God has broken every fetter and I'm not bound anymore." Women who used to be so mean that nobody could live with them are now sweet and patient and understanding and gracious; and men who once cursed and swore and blasphemed now walk along the street memorizing Scriptures as they go on their way to church and prayer meeting.

The Lamb of God, the seed of Abraham, David's greater son, the Lamb that was slain—He specializes in hard cases and He takes away sin—yours and mine. He forgiveth iniquity and pardoneth sin. You confess it; He forgives it. You name it; He destroys it. You expose it; He removes it. You own it; He takes it out. You do not have to have a priest or a preacher, or a baptismal font or a river, or a course in theology; you just have to believe what I am telling you now. Behold the Lamb of God that taketh away the sins of the world. That is where to look, to the Lamb of God. To Jesus, the Lamb of God.

7

WHAT REALLY MATTERS TO GOD?

For God so loved the world, that he gave his only begotten Son, that whosoever believeth in him should not perish, but have everlasting life.

JOHN 3:16

As far as I can remember, I have never preached a sermon on John 3:16, nor have I devoted an entire article or essay to it. It is not that I do not like the text, for I do; it is simply that the text has been too big for me. I have instinctively quoted this often in times of prayer and testimony and writing and preaching.

I was beginning to feel a little uncomfortable about this and confused as to why I could not get a handle on this text; and then I was reading one of Charles J. Ellicott's noble old commentaries of a hundred or more years ago. When the wise old saint of God came to John 3:16, he said something to this effect: "I don't tend to say much about this text; it is a favorite of young preachers, but older preachers feel that it's better felt than talked about. So I'm going to confine my comments on this text to the minimum." And he did.

I knew exactly what he meant and began understanding my reluctance in tackling this text. I believe more than ever that anyone attempting to deal with John 3:16 undertakes an almost insurmountable task, requiring a great deal of sympathy and a generous love for God and men. No person should do this hastily

This text should be approached as Moses approached the burning bush in his day. It is a sacred confrontation with God. As you recall, Moses was required to remove his sandals as he approached this burning bush. Whatever that act meant, like Moses, we must approach this text with unhurried solicitude.

So, I approach this text as one who is filled with great fear, great fascination and an overwhelming sense of inadequacy, almost a despair at the thought of the presence of God before me.

It is hard to find anything to compare with this 25-word text. To me it is as a diamond expertly cut by craftsmen. In order for a diamond to be made, it must crystallize under tremendous pressure. It does not take much for me to put this text in that category. This text has come under the tremendous pressure of the triune God to such a point that it has been crystallized into a shining diamond of truth. A truth so powerful that its brilliance dazzles the believing heart.

You can search the libraries in all the world and search through every book of every language under the sun and you will never find any 25-word text that compares to John 3:16. Even if you would collect all of the great minds of all of the philosophers and thinkers and writers from the beginning of time and put them in one room together, all their combined talents could not produce a text that means so much to the human race. I do not say this as a very young preacher might carelessly say it; I say it thoughtfully and with great conviction after a lifetime of reading, thinking and praying.

Each Person Matters to God

What is the message of John 3:16? And why is this verse of Scripture so highly valuable before all humanity? What message does it bring to us?

I think that the essential part of the New Testament evangel is here: "God so loved the world" (John 3:16). The preacher can take that phrase, run with it from now until the return of Christ and never run out of words to say about it. It is so highly important that this message be conveyed to the ends of the earth.

To boil it down into the familiar terms and words we can understand, I can restate this phrase by simply saying it means *I mean something to God*. Once that phrase is stated, nothing more needs to be said. That sums up in compressed, pressurized fashion the whole intent of the Bible, from Genesis to Revelation.

When I read those words "God so loved the world," it means in personal terms that I mean something to God. God has His eyes upon me and is emotionally concerned about me. If this simple message could rise above the confusion of the religious world, it would offer hope to those who embrace it.

Right here I see a strange paradox—a strange contradiction in human nature. You often see a man walking around as if he is the king of the world. His persona is full of offensive egotism and he is strutting around like a pigeon with his chest bulging outward. Yet when you get to know that man, deep inside, he is filled with a great sense of loneliness and lostness. The thought that plagues his heart and his soul is that nobody really cares about him. Echoing throughout the inner chambers of his heart are the words, "I matter to nobody. Nobody cares about me."

When Jesus said, "Come unto me, all ye that labour and are heavy laden, and I will give you rest" (Matt. 11:28), He was not inviting tired people to Him, although tired people are welcome to come. He was not inviting those who were economically oppressed, though they are also welcome. Nor was He inviting those who had been politically oppressed, as the Jews were under the Romans. Rather, He invited those who are inwardly tired and emotionally fatigued with the heavy pressure of the knowledge, or at least the belief, that in the vast universe, they do not matter to anybody, and nobody actually cares about them. There is no one emotionally concerned with them. There we have this strange paradox tearing at the human heart.

On one side is an egoism that is offensive and rank and makes a man boast and lie and strut. On the other hand, deep within him, is a whimpering, frightened, homesick, heartsick, broken boy who knows that there is nobody in the universe who is emotionally concerned about him. He does not matter to anybody.

Satan's Lie

According to the Scripture, we were made by God with tremendous intellectual and spiritual proportions. We have been made in the image of God. The thing that has destroyed this potential has been sin. It is this that brings us to a sense of orphanage. As a consequence of this, the devil takes advantage of us and whispers his lie into the ear of man: "You do not really matter to God. God does not have any emotional connection with you. God isn't concerned about you."

And we believe that lie.

The poet William Cullen Bryant, in his poem "The Rivulet," set forth this strange paradox. When he returned at 80 years of age to his boyhood home and saw his name carved in his crude boy's lettering, he smiled and wrote this beautiful poem:

And when the days of boyhood came,
And I had grown in love with fame,
Duly I sought thy banks, and tried
My first rude numbers by thy side.
Words cannot tell how bright and gay
The scenes of life before me lay.
Then glorious hopes, that now to speak
Would bring the blood into my cheek,
Passed o'er me; and I wrote, on high,
A name I deemed should never die.

Despite the lamentation of the poet, it did mean something to somebody; he meant something to somebody, and that somebody is God.

Today the world is engulfed in what I refer to as a great hour of humanism. All of humanity has been lumped into one great pile. We hear about statistics to such a point that individualism does not really matter. If you look at all the statistics and come up with the average person, it would be nobody. When God created humanity, he made them of every color and race. In Sunday School, we sing a little song, "Jesus loves the little children, all the children of the world, red and yellow, black and white, they are precious in His sight . . ."

But if you take the law of statistics and average it all out, you end up with nothing. What this statistical nonsense does is do away with the individual. The organization means everything; the individual means nothing at all.

This is the lie of Satan.

If you read the Gospels and follow the life and ministry of Jesus, you will note that He always called individuals to follow Him. The masses followed Him for the "loaves and fishes" that He provided. But Jesus called individuals to come and follow Him. These individuals mattered to Him. Not as a collective mass, but as individuals created in the image of God, His Father. The woman taken in adultery, the mother with her crippled baby, Nicodemus who came to Him by night, and the list goes on and on.

During His ministry, Jesus dealt in individuals, not in statistics. The Christian message reflects that. God does not love masses, He loves people; He loves them individually.

Satan's lie undercuts that truth and has convinced a whole generation of this tremendous lie. Men and women everywhere live under the shadow of this lie that God does not care about them. This deep feeling planted in us by the devil that we do not matter to anybody is confirmed by observation. All you have to do is look around you and find that nature appears to be very little concerned with the individual—concerned with the species, but very little concern about the individual. Alfred Tennyson said the following of nature:

Are God and Nature then at strife
That Nature lends such evil dreams?

So careful of the type she seems,
So careless of the single life.

So nature has planted deep within every normal human being a tremendous urge for self-propagation, and that urge begins
in babyhood and stays with us until we die. That urge guarantees
the perpetuation of the race, and yet when the individual has per-
petuated his kind, he dies and goes back to dust. And there is not
a spot anywhere but that is tainted or blessed, as you like, with
the dust of men where once they had been and are no more. As
William Cullen Bryant stated in his poem "Thanatopsis":

All that tread
The globe are but a handful to the tribes
That slumber in its bosom.—Take the wings
Of morning, pierce the Barcan wilderness,
Or lose thyself in the continuous woods
Where rolls the Oregon, and hears no sound,
Save his own dashings—yet the dead are there:

Since the long flight of years began, matron, maid, soldier
and old man in the gray bloom of old age, and kings and learned
men and fools and wise men all lie down together and the dead
reign there alone. Nature seems to confirm the idea that you
and I do not matter in the great vast universe.

Who cares about the past generation? If you want to check
on that, go out to a cemetery and look around. Who is alive to
care about the old man there? There he lies, dead 200 years.
Who is alive to care about him? His great-, great-, great-, great-

grandchildren? They carelessly come with their camera and, between jokes and wisecracks, snap old great-, great-, great-, great-grandfather's bent and leaning stone that tells where he lies. Who cares about him? He has rolled around in earth's diurnal turns with rocks and stones and trees, and he matters no more than the rocks on the hillside. Few there are that care when we live, and fewer still when we die, and then nobody cares.

Come Just as You Are

Contradicting this lie of Satan, the Christian message boasts, "God cares about you as an individual. No matter what the circumstances around your life at the present, God still cares about you."

I will make a little confession here. Whenever I get the feeling that I'm important, and I speak and preach to a lot of important people, I do something to humble myself. Often I will go into the inner city of Chicago to some of the old rescue missions and preach to the bums, the addicts and the homeless that gather there. As I look out over my ragtag congregation, I see individuals who have lost the sense of their individuality. They are caught up in the sociological statistics of their day.

There is a tramp in the second row. He is dressed in old ragged clothes that do not fit him too well. The shoes do not have laces in them and the one toe seems to be sticking out. He probably has not had a bath for a long time and reeks of dirt and cooties. There he is, smelling of every place he has been the last 10 years.

If I could catch him at a sober moment, I think he might say, "Why am I here? Nobody cares; I don't mean anything to anybody. There isn't anybody, anywhere, who has any emotional concern about me."

And to be truthful about it, his father's gone, his mother's gone, his family will not have anything more to do with him for various reasons. Everybody tries to forget that he is even alive. When the police officers find him lying in the alley, they say, "Move on, buddy."

There he sits, in a deep sense of sadness and orphanage with nothing to live for and nobody to care if he dies. He means nothing to anybody; nobody is concerned about his welfare; nobody cares what happens to him.

But that is not the end of the story. It does not have to stop here. The Christian evangel says, "For God so loved the world."

It says, you—dirt and whiskers and smell and filth—wait a minute. Somebody is emotionally concerned about you. Somebody is not happy because you are the way you are. Somebody even knows your name, remembers you and loves you. You mean something to somebody.

Although our tramp may shake his foggy head in disbelief, the Christian message can get to him. "God so loved you that He gave His only begotten Son that whoever would—and you are included—believe in Him should not perish but have everlasting life. I am here from God to tell you that you do matter. Somebody cares about you."

This is that high compression, that shining facet of the diamond of truth, which God has thrown out to the world almost with happy carelessness and said, "Take it."

Let us take this another step. What about one of our wounded soldiers? It would be hard to find anybody who

experiences the loneliness of heart like our soldiers on the battlefield. What about the one who was wounded and left behind
by his company? There he lies, wounded in enemy country, surrounded by people who speak a language he cannot understand, surrounded by those who would kill him on sight. There
he lies bloody on the hard frozen ground, believing everybody
has forgotten him and forsaken him.

Nothing could be more frightening and discouraging than
that. All hope is gone. Nobody knows or remembers or cares.

I was a number to Uncle Sam, he thinks as he shivers in the
cold of the night. *Now nobody cares . . . nobody.*

Even in the darkness of the night, the Christian message
comes and says, "Somebody does care about you. Maybe you
were only a number to the Army, but you are a living, breathing
human being made in the image of God, and the God in whose
image you are made, cares. You amount to something to God.
You are a treasure to God. You matter."

I can imagine in that last lonely hour, when a sense of orphanage grips the heart, some Bible verse that he had memo-
rized in Sunday School seems to appear from somewhere deep
within him. The memory of that verse begins to open up his
heart. "Oh, God, when I was a boy in Sunday School they told
me I mattered. Is it any different now? Have You changed Your
mind, God? Is it any different now that I'm a man?"

Then somewhere buried deep in the halls of memory comes
the ancient voice of God, saying, "No, I'm still not happy about
your condition, for I so loved you that I gave My only begotten
Son that whosoever believes in Him should not perish but have
everlasting life."

In the light of that verse, the lies of Satan begin to disintegrate and the Christian message permeates the heart of the wounded, abandoned soldier who is lying on the battlefield about to die.

Let us leave that wounded soldier and look in upon his mother. It is quite possible that many mothers grieve over their sons who they believe are in hell. They do not have the comfort of knowing that those sons will greet them on that happy day. They do not know that the lie of Satan can be broken by the memory of that one verse.

The mother of the thief on the cross weeps within herself and says, "I have failed him; society has failed him; and he's failed society. My boy, my boy." What she did not know was that the One who cared was within touching distance of her boy. That outcast, that rebel traitor, turned his eyes at the very last moment to the One who cared, and said, "Lord, remember me when thou comest into thy kingdom." And Jesus said, "Verily I say unto thee, To day shalt thou be with me in paradise" (Luke 23:42-43).

The only thing the mother had was the knowledge that her son died by execution. What she did not know was that the One who cared for him had reached out and touched him. What a happy reunion that must have been when the thief on the cross in paradise embraced his mother! It is only something I imagine in my mind, but I can appreciate the joy that such a reunion would be.

The Christian message says, "God so loved," and that love is not for a species, but for individuals. God loves people. We sing the hymn with the words, "Jesus, lover of *my* soul," not "Jesus, lover of the human race."

In one strict sense, there is no human race. The human race is composed of individuals; and if you take away the individuals, you will have no human race. And there is such a thing as a crowd; but in another sense, there is no such a thing as a crowd. A crowd is simply a congregation of individuals; and every individual has eternal significance and meaning in the heart of God. "God so loved." God is emotionally concerned with the individual.

All around the world, we can go and tell them—the shipwrecked sailor, the chronic failure, the man who fails at everything he touches. Some people have success at the ends of their fingers, they just have to touch it and it turns to gold. Other people are chronic failures; they have established a pattern of failure. They add up two times two, and it ends up to five. Nothing they do succeeds. For them it is failure all the way, and they say, "I fail at everything, I'm just no good."

English is such a humorously downright blunt and accurate language. "He's no good," they say. And those words just mean everything. A couple of women will say about another woman, "She's no good."

Take in the whole United States of America, spill over into Canada, down into Mexico, across the ocean to Europe and on to Asia, take them all in. There is not one human being about which God says, "He's no good." He says, "There's none righteous, no not one"; we all must be saved, and we will all perish if we do not repent and be born again. But in the sense of being written off as no good and hopeless, thank God, there is nobody.

Do not listen to any of these interpreters of truth who say God has chosen some and not chosen others, and that the ones He has chosen are good and the ones that He has not chosen are no good. They are vessels of wrath fitted to destruction, and God created them to have the fun of damning them. There is nobody like that in the universe. I do not say there is good in everybody, but I do say there is somebody that likes him or her, whether he or she is good or not. There is somebody emotionally concerned about him or her. Everybody matters to God. God is concerned about individuals.

But you say, "If you knew me, you wouldn't talk like that." I do not know you, of course, but it would not make any difference, it is still true. God is concerned about you.

You say, "Yes, concerned about the human race."

No, concerned about *you*.

"Concerned about my family?"

No, concerned about you as well as your family.

But you say, "I've sinned; I've lied; I've failed; I've made vows that I've broken; I've made promises and failed to keep them; I'm no good."

All I can say to you is that if you persist in your gloomy unbelief, then there is nothing even God can do for you. Because it is unbelief that tells you at the same time your heart is swollen with pride that another part of your heart says, "There is no use, I'm no good." God Almighty went to all the trouble to say that you are. Not that you are good morally, but you are some good to God, because God is going to make you over. He has proven that He cares by sending His only begotten Son that whosoever believes in Him should not perish but have everlasting life.

I can only point to this: "So then faith cometh by hearing, and hearing by the word of God" (Rom. 10:17), and it begins to work as we begin to affirm this truth. If you would begin to affirm, to say to God, "Oh God, believing Thy Word, I affirm that I mean something to You," it might change the whole complexion of your life for all the years to come.

"I'm a sinner, but I matter. I'm hell-bound, but I'm not going to hell with nobody caring about me. I matter even though I'm all alone. I'm a number to the government, but the God of the universe says that I matter."

If your heart believes that, for that is part of the Christian evangel, then you begin to pray. Faith cometh by hearing and faith becomes perfect by praying, "Oh, God, I believe I matter to Thee." You see how simple it is and how easy it is to come into the arms of God, to come back to God, if you have wandered away?

We come to Him the first time as a sinner with the full confidence that God has taken the great truth—the truth the devil never discovered, the truth that mankind never dreamed of discovering—and compressed it by all the pressure of the triune God into the shining diamond of truth and held it up as the church's message. "For God so loved the world, that he gave his only begotten Son, that whosoever believeth in him should not perish, but have everlasting life" (John 3:16).

If you have sinned and have not come to Christ believing, and have not surrendered, it is not all right. You shall perish most surely. But no matter how bad or how far away from God you are or how often you have failed Him or how many lies you have told Him—how terrible you have been or how no good you feel you are—I have the word for you: You do matter. God is concerned; God is not happy about you; He says, "Come and let whoever hear it say come and whoever will let him come."

Those that have known you, known your dirty temper, known your impossible disposition, known your past and have no faith in you, they cannot keep you out, for they do not have the keys of death and hell. They cannot keep you out. Because there is One to whom you matter so much that He gave His only begotten Son. In the words of Charlotte Elliott, "Just as I am, without one plea, but that Thy blood was shed for me, and that Thou bidst me come to Thee, O Lamb of God, I come, I come."

8

The Personal Application of Christ's Coming Into the World

For God sent not his Son into the world to condemn the world;
but that the world through him might be saved.

John 3:17

This verse makes three related statements so meaningful, so momentous and so critically important to the human race that in the most conservative language, we may properly say of this verse that it constitutes a *proclamation extraordinary*. First, God sent His Son into the world. Second, He did not send Him to condemn the world. Third, He sent Him in order that the world might be saved.

To show you that I do not read anything into it, that I am merely showing you what is there, look at Charles B. Williams's translation. He puts it in the positive instead of the negative. The meaning is precisely the same: "For God sent his Son into the world, not to pass sentence on it, but that the world through him might be saved" (John 3:17).

Let me ask you to do something ridiculous. Think away this verse. It does not exist. God never spoke it. It was never recorded in the Holy Scriptures. Moreover, it does not look out at us as the proclamation extraordinary. Once that is done, I can understand why many Christian people are filled with apathy and indifference to the world around them. Now, I can understand the frivolous nature of many church activities. How else can you explain this except doing away with this verse?

If this verse does not exist, I could understand why people could come to church and sit in stoic silence. I could understand why people could kneel in prayer and mumble into a deaf ear that does not hear us. I could understand why we could rise in the morning and be more concerned that the newspaper had arrived than with whether this verse was here or not. If the verse was not here, I could understand our apathy and explain our indifference. But this verse is here, proclaiming the intent of God.

I could say it is the indifference of despair. Israel understood this sort of despair. In Egypt, for 400 years, generation had followed generation in slavery and bondage. When a new generation of Israel came up, they did not expect anything but bondage. They languished in a prison camp for so many years without hope of ever having it otherwise. So their jaws hung slack, their shoulders were bent and they had no expectation.

David the psalmist expressed their feelings in a psalm: "By the rivers of Babylon, there we sat down, yea, we wept, when we remembered Zion. We hanged our harps upon the willows in the midst thereof. For there they that carried us away captive required of us a song; and they that wasted us required of us mirth, saying, Sing us one of the songs of Zion. How shall we sing the LORD's song in a strange land?" (Ps. 137:1-4).

They had definitely given up to despair, with no expectation of any change.

If this proclamation extraordinary had not been made, I could understand how we could be so unhappy. I could understand how the human race could walk around looking down at the earth like the beasts and rarely looking at the sky. But in the light of the fact that this verse was made a reality 2,000 years ago, I ask this question: What is the matter with us? What is the matter with Christians, and what is the matter with the unsaved man who has the message?

This verse does exist. God did speak it. And it looks out at us from the Holy Scriptures, indeed, as the proclamation extraordinary. It carries with it the very heartbeat of God Himself.

In the full sound of this proclamation—more gravely significant than any declaration of law or proclamation of peace, any plague or any news from afar, any discovery of any new continent or even a new world, none of which could compare with this—people are indifferent. Upon our eyes there seems to have fallen a strange dimness, and on our ears a strange dullness, and in our minds a stupor, and in our hearts, I am afraid, a great callousness. In reading this over and thinking about it and seeing the brilliant shining quality of it and the significance of it to the human race, we are so little stirred up about it. It is so wonderful and yet so terrible that this verse should be here.

A Score for the Enemy

I believe this apathy upon us is a technical victory for organized evil. I do not know too much about the dark spirits that move up and down in the world. I know as much as I want to know. I want to know even less as I get nearer to God in grace, but I know the Bible teaches that there are sinister spirits that walk up and down. There are even organized spirits. Perhaps that is what it means when Paul talks about principalities and powers and mights and dominions (see Eph. 1:21). It does not mean the good ones, so it must mean the opposite ones. They are undoubtedly abroad, invisible to the naked eye, perhaps even inaudible to the ear, but they are abroad. They are the legions of hell; they are "the fifth column" of iniquity present in the world; their business is to subvert and destroy and bind and kill like the thief that got into the fold. It is a technical victory for the devil; and I believe it is more than that.

This proclamation extraordinary must be of great astonishment to the unfallen creatures we read about in the Scriptures; the watchers, the holy ones, the seraphim, the cherubim, the angels, the archangels and the holy creatures that never fell. I am not sure what they know, but they must know something. Some had been sent to announce the birth of Jesus. Some to announce the resurrection of Jesus; and in another instance, in the book of Revelation, we see them flying in mid-heaven, moving about among men, so they must be there or here. How much they know and understand is beyond my ability to comprehend.

If they know what we know about this proclamation extraordinary, their minds must be filled with great wonder and astonishment. And perhaps they even wonder at how men and women can look at this with such indifference.

How can educated Christians, with Bibles in every room of the house, be so apathetic to the import of this verse of Scripture? This must astonish those holy creatures.

When we read "God sent not his Son into the world to condemn the world" (John 3:17) with apathy and indifference, it is not a true reflection of our culture, but proof of our sin, and proof that we are more hardened.

This is not only a victory for organized evil, and astonishment to unfallen creatures, but it is a great grief to God on high. I believe God loved them too. Not the enthusiasm of fanaticism, but I believe God loved them.

In the Gospel record, we see that Jesus had a special fondness for babies. I think it was because they are so vigorous, buoyant, unsophisticated and fresh. They just do what they do out of simplicity and to an immediate response of their young hearts. And the Lord must have loved them; He laid his hands on their heads and said, "for of such is the kingdom of heaven" (Matt. 19:14), and made a great deal of the babies.

Ever since, theologians have been tossing and kicking these babies around, wanting to know what it all means. Simplehearted people know that Jesus just loved babies, and that is all. He loved the bald ones, the hairy ones, the redheads and all the rest of them, because there was something about them that had not yet been spoiled.

William Wordsworth said this in the fifth stanza of his poem "Intimations of Immortality":

Our birth is but a sleep and a forgetting:
The Soul that rises with us, our life's Star,

Hath had elsewhere its setting,
And cometh from afar:
Not in entire forgetfulness,
And not in utter nakedness,
But trailing clouds of glory do we come
From God, who is our home:
Heaven lies about us in our infancy!

We come fresh from the hand of God and trailing clouds of glory, and a little bit of heaven lies around the growing boy. As he travels further from his home, sad and tragic as it may be, the glory disappears and evaporates and that little bit of heaven that lies around the newborn boy disappears like dew before the sun. Finally, it is no heaven anymore and no glory anymore; but he forgets God, and his heart is hard and the door shuts around him and he is a carnal man in a fallen world.

This sort of thing has even affected the sanctuary on Sunday morning. It is quite unusual for anybody to come to church on a Sunday with their guard down and their heads bowed, saying, "We are before you to hear what God will speak to us." Any pastor who has that kind of a congregation is richly endowed with God's blessing.

But I am afraid that it is not too common. The average Christian today has become so learned and so worldly and so sophisticated and so blasé and so burned out and so bored and so religiously tired and so beat up that the freshness and delighted trails from clouds of glory seem to have gone. And it is the great need of this hour. A verse like John 3:17 should have an instant response in the human breast.

Why should God send this proclamation extraordinary, "God sent not His Son into the world to condemn the world"? What was the purpose behind it all? He did not send His Son to condemn the world, but that the world might be saved. And the sad thing is that many Christians take it with such apathy. Who has poisoned our cup? What evil alliances have we made? What has sin been doing to our hearts? What devil has been working on the strings of the harp of our soul? Who has been giving us sedatives? Who has been feeding us the medicine of apathy? What has happened to us that we can talk about this, sing about this, preach about this, and it leaves us untouched?

I sympathize with William Wordsworth when he said he would rather be a heathen, believe in a heathen creed and stand on the shore of the ocean and imagine that he could hear old Neptune or old Triton blow his horn and have something alive than to be a civilized Christian to which everything has died. It may be an extreme statement, but I think I know what he meant. The world is too much with us. We have wasted our powers in getting and spending.

What Distinguishes the Proclamation Extraordinary

What is it about this proclamation extraordinary that separates it from any and all other proclamations? Where would you go to find something equal to this? And why should this proclamation grip our hearts and minds so firmly?

I propose that nothing like this exists in the world today. The proclamation of independence as perpetrated by our founding fathers was, in the grand scheme of things, quite important. We are today what we are because of this grand proclamation. As important and powerful as this is, it pales in comparison to God's proclamation extraordinary.

Our founding fathers were great in many regards. We can name them all here. But when we come to this proclamation extraordinary, we have someone greater than Thomas Jefferson, George Washington or Benjamin Franklin—greater than all of those founding fathers put together.

Maybe in the future something will come that will be newer and grander proclamations of God based on this one. But now there is nothing in all of the world throughout Scripture as great as this proclamation.

The proclamation begins with God sending His Son into the world for the purpose of saving the world. "God sent His Son into the world." I need to take one word and change it so that it means exactly what God meant. The word "world" does not mean geography. The proclamation is not, "He sent His Son into the Near East . . . He sent His Son into Palestine . . . into Bethlehem . . . into the corner of Second and Ninth Streets." The word "world" does not have any geographical or astronomical meaning. It has nothing to do with kilometers and distances and continents and islands. It does not refer to space, topography, mountains and towns. Of course, He came to Palestine; He came to Bethlehem, and certainly, He came to that little land that lies between the seas.

But that is not what is meant here by the word "world." That is not why He came. "God sent His Son into the world," not "He sent His Son into the near East." It is not "God so loved geography." It is not "God so loved the snowcapped mountains or the sun-kissed meadows or the flowering streams or the great ice peaks to the north." God may love all of them. I rather think He does. Many passages in the Psalms give us the idea that God is in love with the world He created. But that is not what it means here. God sent His Son into the human race. Jesus Christ came to people. And not just to one race of people, but to all humanity. These other things are only incidental. It is people He came to, and He came to save them.

Imagine if we could take a bird's-eye view of the entire world at one glance. Suppose we could be a star looking down upon the vast sea of humanity. What would we see? We would see the crippled, the blind and the lepers. We would see the fat, the lean, the tall and the short. We would see the dirty and the clean. We would see them walking the Avenue bold and upright without fearing any police officer. We also would see them scuttling the back alleys and crawling through windows. We would see them twisting and twitching in the last agonies of death. We would see them kicking footballs over the fields and running around the baseball track. We would see them tiny and sick and great and strong. We would see them ignorant, not able to put one letter behind the other. We would see them walking gravely under the elms in some college town, dreaming deep dreams of a fourth dimension, or dreaming up some great poem or play to astonish and delight the world.

We would see people. Plain people, black people, people whose eyes slant different from ours, people whose hair is not like our hair at all. People whose diets are not like ours. People with customs unlike our habits, and very different from us; but we would see people. Their differences are external; their similarities are internal. Their differences would be customs and habits, and their likenesses would have to do with nature. The human nature Jesus Christ came to rescue.

So they would be there as the thief and the liar. They would be there as the martyr, the mother of a dying soldier and the boy on the stretcher that was sent away with the sound of the "Star Spangled Banner," to be forgotten out of the hospital. They are people, nevertheless, and God sent His Son to the people. He is the people's Savior. Jesus Christ came to people like your family and mine and other people like us.

Not only to the learned theologians, to men who can spout Greek and Hebrew. Jesus came to them too—their ability to read Greek and Hebrew is only incidental. What they are is the same as the ignorant boy whose language simply will not order itself. You scratch a professor and you find a hillbilly. Take a pin or a knife blade and prick the skin a little of that dignified woman, the carefully groomed egotist walking around with an elitist book under her arm, on her way to hear some opera. Prick her a little and she is just one more squawking woman.

Reclaiming What Is His

How would you define the mission of Christ when He came into this world? Let us say, for example, that we have never heard the gospel. We do not have a Bible or hymnbook. The 2,000 years of Christian tradition is gone and we do not consider that. We have never heard the message of salvation. We are like the pagans who live unto themselves without any thought of God.

With this scenario, what would be the first thing we would do upon hearing this marvelous proclamation from Christ?

The proclamation of God sending His Son into the world to redeem the world? What would be our response to that?

I am sure it would be similar to what Adam and Eve did in the Garden of Eden. They ran for the rocks and the trees to hide from the proclamation. There was something within them striking fear and terror and sending them in a panic to hide.

With that in mind, what is the logical mission for this coming One? Well, our own hearts tell us why. Sin, darkness, deception and moral disease all tell us why. The lies we have told. The temper tantrums we have thrown. The jealousies we have felt. All this tells us why He should have come. The sin we cannot deny tells us why He should have come. That mission was to judge the world. If He had not told us that, the Holy Ghost would never have said not to judge the world. Why did He say that? Because He knew the human conscience could only say one thing: "Oh, God, if You're sending Someone from Your throne, find a place for me to hide, for my heart tells me I ought to die. My heart tells me that I've piled up sin, and I should be sentenced to die. And if this righteous One is coming, then I ought to die."

However, that was not His mission. He did not come to judge us. The proclamation extraordinary is simply, He sent His Son into the world, but not to judge the world. That was not His purpose at all. He came that men might be saved. He did not come to condemn, but to reclaim. That was the mission of our Lord Jesus Christ. He came to reclaim that which was rightfully His by creation.

Another question might be asked: Why did He come to men and not the fallen angels? I think the reason is obvious. He

came to men and not to angels because man had been origi-
nally created in the image of God, and angels had not. He came
to fallen Adam's brood and not to that of the fallen angels, because Adam had once been made in the image of God. It was a
morally logical thing when Jesus became incarnated. He could
become incarnated in the flesh because God made man in His
own image. Christ had the potentialities that could take the
Incarnation. God Almighty could pull the blanket of human
flesh up around His ears. He could be a man to walk among
men. But there was nothing of like kind among angels and
fallen creatures other than man. So He came not to condemn
but to reclaim.

You Can Take It Personally

When you read, "God sent not his Son into the world to condemn the world" (John 3:17), think in personal terms. The
cross is not mentioned in John 3:17, and the cross is not mentioned in John 3:16. We sometimes imagine that we have to
open our mouths and in one great big sentence say all the theology there is to say. God is not so squeamish. He says it all
somewhere in the Book, and the cross stands out like a great,
bright, shining pillar in the middle of the Scriptures. Without
that cross on which the Savior died there could be no Scripture,
no revelation, no redemption. But He did not say anything
about the cross here. He simply said He sent His Son and He
gave His Son—those two words, "sent" and "gave." He gave His
Son, He sent His Son. Later the text develops the truth that in
giving His Son, He gave Him to die on the cross; but He did not
say so here.

Think of this in personal terms. Christ taught us to do this in the story of the prodigal son, the most pathos-filled story ever told by mortal man. God was afraid we would get generic and theological with it all and put it into a book, put a period down there and have an article one, section two, subdivision B.

God knew man's propensity, so we have the story of the prodigal son (see Luke 15:11-32). It is so well known that it does not need repeating here. But in that story, we have the history of all humanity. No matter what culture you go into there is some story of a prodigal son.

The essence of the prodigal son is the focus on "me." The son only thought about things that affected him personally. No thought was given to the world around him but only as it related to him personally and immediately. According to the Scriptures, this prodigal son "came to himself" (Luke 15:17). When he saw what the world was doing to him personally, he remembered his father's house. If only people today would understand that everything in the world is against them, they would come to their senses, so to speak, and find their way back to the Father's house.

When the prodigal son found the courage to go back to the father's house, he discovered, much to his surprise, his father waiting to receive him with open arms. He found his father excited about his return. David understood this and wrote, "The LORD is my shepherd; I shall not want" (Ps. 23:1). He did not say, "The Lord is one's shepherd, one shall not want; one can lie down in green pastures." It would not mean anything because it would not have been personal. He said, "*My* shepherd, *I* shall not want, he maketh *me* to lie down."

The prodigal son could have said, "One's father has goods enough and to spare, and one perishes with hunger; one should arise and go unto one's father." That is general and makes it religious, but it does not amount to anything. The prodigal son said, "I'm the hungry boy, God's my Father, and my father is back home; I'm going back home." He made it personal.

Unbelief always hides behind three trees. Here they are, "somewhere else," "some other time," "somebody else." Somebody hears a sermon on John 3:16 and says, "Somewhere else it's true; on somebody else it's true; some other time it's true, but not now." That is a hideous lie of unbelief.

Faith rises up in belief in God and about oneself and says, "God sent His Son into the human race that He might redeem the human race. He cannot redeem the human race en masse. He has to redeem and save the human race as individuals. That must mean me. Believe about yourself and say to yourself, *Not somewhere else, but here. Not some other time, but now. Not somebody else, but me.*"

Single yourself out, not somebody else, but you. Jesus Christ came not to condemn you but to save you, knowing your name, knowing all about you, knowing your weight right now, knowing your age, knowing what you do, knowing where you live, knowing what you ate for supper and what you will eat for breakfast, where you will sleep tonight, how much your clothing cost, who your parents were. He knows you individually as though there were not another person in the entire world. He died for you as certainly as if you had been the only lost one. He knows the worst about you and is the One who loves you the most.

If you are out of the fold and away from God, put your name in the words of John 3:16 and say, "Lord, it is I. I'm the cause and reason why Thou didst on earth come to die." That kind of positive, personal faith and a personal Redeemer is what saves you. If you will just rush in there, you do not have to know all the theology and all the right words. You can say, "I am the one He came to die for."

Write it down in your heart and say, "Jesus, this is me—Thee and me," as though there were no others. Have that kind of personalized belief in a personal Lord and Savior. Once that personalization takes place in the human breast they do not fool with that fellow anymore. The Lord God Almighty witnesses within that soul that something has happened there and he belongs to God, and God to him. He no longer needs to be fed like a baby with lukewarm, watered-down milk. He grows in grace because he has had that personalized, individual experience of knowing that John 3:16 means him.

9

Perfect Harmony and Unity in the Trinity

Then answered Jesus and said unto them, Verily, verily, I say unto you,
The Son can do nothing of himself, but what he seeth the Father do:
for what things soever he doeth, these also doeth the Son likewise.

JOHN 5:19

Sam Jones, the eccentric American evangelist of a couple of generations ago, said when the average preacher took a text it reminded him of an insect trying to carry a bale of cotton. And if ever I was trying to lift a bale of cotton, it is right here with the next passage of Scripture in John 5:17-26.

In the opening part of this passage, our Lord explains how He works with the Father. "The Son can do nothing of himself, but what he seeth the Father do: for what things soever he doeth, these also doeth the Son likewise" (John 5:19). I have mentioned the unceasing activity of God the Father, the un-wearied, restless and yet ever restful omnipotent creative work of the Father working toward a predetermined end. Working toward a purpose that He purposed in Christ Jesus before the world began. Here our Lord tells us that His working is in line with the Father's working and altogether dependent upon it. "The Son can do nothing of himself" (v. 19).

This is a bit of theology that we can well take with us into every corridor and passage of the whole Word of God. "The Son can do nothing of himself." But the Son can do everything in Himself. I quoted the old Middle Ages, medieval concept that the Son is not God of Himself, but He is God in Himself. Or correctly wording it, the Son is not God of Himself but of the Father. But He is God in Himself. And here we have it that the Son works Himself, but He does not work of Himself, for He can do nothing of Himself.

There are several wonderful doctrines taught here that should delight the believer. One of them is the harmony in the blessed Godhead.

Coequal and Coeternal

I think it would be impossible to overemphasize this doctrine that there is a perfect harmony between the persons of the Godhead. We must never allow ourselves even once to think there is any conflict or to think any conflict into the persons of the Godhead. The Father planned it, but He planned it in His Son. And He wrought it through His Son through the power of the Holy Spirit. So there has never been anything but harmony in the blessed Godhead. And whatever the Father does, the Son sees Him do and works in harmony with what the Father is doing. And the Holy Ghost is the perfect bond between the Father and the Son, energizing the eternal Son with the energies of the

Father and so working harmoniously to a preordained end. This is taught in this passage and throughout the entire Bible.

But also there is taught the subordinate position of the Son of man. This has bothered some people very much that the Son is equal to the Father and yet is subordinate to the Father, for our Lord Jesus Christ teaches both. He says that the "Son can do nothing of himself" (John 5:19), and He says, "my Father is greater than I" (John 14:28), and so He takes a subordinate position and prays to His Father. An equal does not pray to an equal; an equal prays to one who is above him and to whom he can address his prayers; and when the Son prays to the Father, it is a passive confession of subordination. He is not equal to the Father, so He prays to One who is above Him and yet He can say, "I and my Father are one" (John 10:30), and, "he that hath seen me hath seen the Father" (John 14:9).

Now, what does this mean, and how do we get this way? And is there contradiction there? No, there's no contradiction there, because the old Athanasian Creed has it that as pertaining to His Godhead, "Equal to the Father, as touching His godhead; and inferior to the Father, as touching His manhood; who, although He is God and man, yet he is not two, but one Christ."

And in this ancient and holy trinity there is nothing before and nothing after, nothing higher and nothing lower, but all three persons together, coeternal and coequal. So that Jesus Christ has the two natures, the nature of man and the nature of God, harmonized into one perfect personality. Let us not imagine Jesus as a schizophrenic, one with a split personality. Let us know that He has one personality but two natures harmonized into this one personality. And when He speaks about

Himself as the son of Mary, he says, "The Son can do nothing of himself, but what he seeth the Father do: for what things soever he doeth, these also doeth the Son likewise" (John 5:19), and says, "my Father is greater than I" (John 14:28). When He speaks about Himself as God, He says, "I and my Father are one" (John 10:30). So there is no contradiction here, there is only an understanding.

The Mystery of Three in One

As a very young preacher, I was familiar with the "Jesus Only" group. They claim that the name of the Godhead is Jesus. According to them, the Scriptures say, "Teach all nations, baptizing them in the name of the Father, and of the Son, and of the Holy Ghost" (Matt. 28:19). But it does not give us the name. But Jesus, according to them, is the name of the Father and of the Son and of the Holy Ghost.

The problem is that they cannot see how three can be one and how one can be three. They make their theology with mathematics. Their arithmetic gets them into confusion, so they say there is but one person who is the Godhead, Jesus, and that Jesus is the Father and He is the Son and He is the Holy Ghost. These friends have never explained to me how one can be the Father of another.

They teach that there is only one person of the Godhead and He is Father and Son and Holy Spirit. I cannot see how it could possibly be that the name of these three, or the name of this one, is Jesus. It is also true of a school of modern theologians that there is one person in the Godhead, but He has three masks. That is, He has three faces.

The old god of the ancient Roman days was named Janus. He was the Roman god of gates and doors (*ianua*), beginnings and endings, and is represented with a double-faced head, each looking in opposite directions. But these theologians have gone one further and given the Godhead three faces. When this one person of the Godhead wants to be the Father, he puts on the Father's face and turns that to you. When He wants to be the Son, He turns the Son's face, and when He wants to be the Spirit, He turns the Spirit's face to you. I find it much easier to believe in an ancient, incorruptible, uncreated Godhead, a fountain of ancient Godhead, and the three persons leaping up out of that Godhead.

I have thought of the Godhead as a great sea. The ancient mystic theologians taught that the Godhead goes back of and beneath any of the three persons of the Trinity. They teach that there is the underlying Godhead and that the Godhead expressed Himself as Father, Son and Holy Ghost, in three personalities. That is what I believe. I believe that the Father is the ancient Godhead expressing Himself as the Father, and the Son is the ancient Godhead in expression as the Son, and the Holy Ghost is the ancient Godhead—all of one substance and of one eternity. One, without beginning and without creation. And so we have the triune God.

When Jesus says, "My Father is greater than I," He is speaking of His manhood. When He says, "I and my Father are one," He is speaking of His Godhead. And when He speaks of His Godhead, He does not take any low place beneath the Father, neither does the Holy Spirit; these three are one. It is a wonderful mystery and I do not claim to be able to understand it, but I confess that I delight to tremble before the Throne and say "holy" three times repeated: "holy, holy, holy." So there is a harmony in the blessed Godhead. There is a subordination of the Son to the Father with the purposes of creation and redemption.

Unbroken Fellowship in the Godhead

The third thing this text teaches is the unaffected relation between the Father and the Son in the Incarnation.

I do not hear many preach about the everlasting Godhead and the eternal creed. That is not to reflect on anyone who is preaching the truth, but it is only to say that there certainly is truth being tragically neglected in the day in which we live. And there is a whole world of golden truth that we can mine, with a pickaxe of prayer, from the Bible that will be meat and drink and food and wonderful help to all Christian people.

There was an unaffected relationship between the Father and the Son in the Incarnation. We generally say that Jesus Christ left His home far above and that He came down and cut Himself off from the Father and left the delights of the Father's bosom and the Father's heart and walked in exile among men. But that is only partly true. The hymn by Charles Wesley, "And Can It Be That I Should Gain," sets this before us:

He left his father's throne above,
So free, so infinite his grace,
Emptied himself of all but love,
and bled for Adam's helpless race.

He did do that, but He never emptied Himself of deity. He considered equality with God not something to be held on to, but emptied Himself. Remember one thing: He never emptied Himself of His deity. He could not do it. It would be metaphysically impossible, even to think such a thought that the eternal Son should be anything less than God. But He never emptied Himself of any attributes of deity; rather, He emptied Himself of the accoutrements of deity. He emptied Himself of the evidences of the deity, covered the deity in a cloak of opaque flesh and walked among us as though He were a man. He was God in overalls, living on the earth, wearing the common denim of humanity and covering over His deity. When occasion required, He could let His deity shine through, as once when He prayed to the heavenly Father and His face became shining white and His garments whiter than any flower on earth, shining like the sun as He knelt there. It was only His deity showing itself through the previously opaque veil of His manhood (see Luke 9:28-29).

But even while He walked on earth He was with unbroken fellowship with His Father. For it is impossible that the Father and the Son should ever cease in the ancient sea of the Godhead to be joined together as one. But the man Christ Jesus cried, "My God, my God, why hast thou forsaken me?" (Matt. 27:46). And as pertaining to His manhood, He was forsaken of the Father; but as pertaining to His deity, forsaking would be impossible, for we cannot divide the deity or separate the persons of the holy Trinity. So Jesus, when He walked on earth, saw the Father; and that gives us our forethought, the perfect clairvoyance of the Son.

The Son's Clear View of the Father

I use that word "clairvoyance" without apology though it needs an explanation. What a beautiful word it is: "clairvoyance." I like it because it means clear sight; perfect visibility; perfect, unending seeing with no clouds between. But the cults have taken it and the wizards and witches and spiritualists and now we have clairvoyants used by the spirits. They have no more right to it than I have the right to the title of being called King of England. The truth of the matter is, the spiritualist does not see clearly with perfect visibility and perfect understanding. No one sees clearly but the Son.

"Then answered Jesus and said unto them, Verily, verily, I say unto you, The Son can do nothing of himself, but what he seeth the Father do: for what things soever he doeth, these also doeth the Son likewise" (John 5:19).

The Father and the Son are working harmoniously within sight of each other. Not all the clouds that ever came over Palestine prevented the clairvoyance of the Son, the clear sight of Jesus Christ. And not all the shadows that gathered around Calvary prevented the eternal Son from gazing full into the face of the eternal Father.

As pertaining to His manhood, He cried in agony of sacrifice and offering, "My God, my God," then bled and died as God turned away from the sacrifice. However, the eternal God was unaffected and undivided, and the Son looked into the clear face of the Father without a shadow between. It had to be like that. What a terrible, mixed-up and imperfect redemption it would have been if Jesus Christ had to fight His way through; if He, the eternal Son, had been rejected from the presence of the Father, we would not have had Christianity then, we would have had Roman mythology.

Perfect Love Within the Godhead

Listening to some preaching today, we might imagine there exists in the Godhead some kind of conflict, and that the Son of God was like some demigod of Rome who slipped in and rescued mankind like Prometheus brought down fire from heaven and was punished for his robbery. But nothing like that exists. It is the perfect clairvoyance, the perfect sight of the Son, the clear seeing of Jesus as He walked among men and gazed into the face of the Father, for the Father was there and is here. For He said the Father loves the Son, and this love, of course, is not simply the love of God for a good man, it is the ancient unity of love among the holy Three. That is what it means in the Bible when it says, "And we have known and believed the love that God hath to us. God is love; and he that dwelleth in love dwelleth in God, and God in him" (1 John 4:16).

"For as the Father raiseth up the dead, and quickeneth them; even so the Son quickeneth whom he will" (John 5:21). If this means anything at all, it means that the working of the Son in regeneration is as radical and miraculous as the working of the Father in raising the dead. It means that as the Father raises the dead and quickens them, even so the Son quickens whom He will. It is in the present tense and is not talking about the Resurrection. He is talking about the present time: "The hour is coming, and now is, when the dead shall hear the voice of the Son of God: and they that hear shall live" (John 5:25).

So, He is not talking about future resurrections but about the present time, and He says that as the Father has the ability to raise the dead and give them life, so He has given to the Son power to raise the dead and give them life. Only the Father raises the dead in the future resurrection; the Son raises the dead right now. The work of Christ in making a Christian is as radical a thing as raising Lazarus from the dead. When Lazarus came out of the tomb a live man where a dead man had been, he stood everlastingly as a figure of a Christian who stands up a live man where a dead man has been, a clean man where a filthy man has been.

There is a harmony in the blessed Godhead, an unaffected relationship between the Father and the Son, because of the perfection going into the Son, and He sees as He has from eternity the Father at work. And because the Father loves the Son, and because the Father has given into the hands of the Son power to raise the dead, even as He raises the dead, all men should honor the Son even as they honor the Father. And He said, if we withhold honor from the Son, we withhold honor from the Father also. That is the plain teaching of the Scriptures.

I know there are those who do not honor the Son. They honor Him only as a good teacher, perhaps the best, but only a good teacher and preacher of the Word. But, the Scripture says all men should honor the Son as they honor the Father. So you need have no hesitation in attributing all of the worship and glory to the Son that you attribute to the Father. You need have no fear, because the Father lives for the glory of the Son, and the Son lives for the glory of the Father, and the Spirit of God lives for the glory of the Father and Son. So we honor the Son of God. We have no hesitation whatsoever in praying to the Son as we pray also to the Father; and while it is not usually done, we also have no hesitation in addressing the Holy Ghost.

The One to Whom We Pray

About here, somebody might ask about praying to the Holy Spirit. Is it ever the right thing to do? Should we ever pray to the Spirit? My answer is that normally we pray to the Father in the name of the Son and in the Spirit, but Jesus Christ had no hesitation in receiving prayers and granting them when He walked among men. So obviously, there is no formula. If there had been an unbreakable formula that the only way to pray would be to pray to the Father in the name of the Son, then why should Jesus have broken that order and allowed prayer to be made to Himself?

Plainly then, the persons of the Godhead are equal to God and the persons of the Godhead are equally present before our minds when we pray. When we sing the lyrics of the hymn "Faithful Guide"—"Holy Spirit, faithful Guide, ever near the Christian's side"—(Marcus M. Wells), we are praying to the Spirit. When we pray, "Holy Ghost, with light divine, shine upon this heart of mine; chase the shades of night away, turn the darkness into day" (Andrew Reed), we are praying to the Spirit.

In the Bible, you will find instances where men prayed to the Holy Ghost. "Awake, O north wind; and come, thou south; blow upon my garden, that the spices thereof may flow out. Let my beloved come into his garden, and eat his pleasant fruits" (Song of Songs 4:16). Normally, prayers are made to the persons of the Trinity—to the Father in the name of the Son, but also, without harm and any transgression of the Scriptures, through the Son when you want to pray to the Son. If in prayer or song to the Holy Ghost, then also to the Holy Ghost.

God is never jealous for a formula. Religious people are. They live and die by formula. They put it one, two, three, four and if you say one, two, four, three, they will leap all over you and with white-faced anger prove they love truth because they are so mad. And they love the beautiful order of the truth, and if you said four before you said three, they hate you for your heresy. They love the truth so much.

Always remember that God is easy to get along with, and if your heart is right, He is not too concerned about the formula. God is kind and good and gracious, because there are some of us that are just too hard to get along with. If God were as hard to get along with as we are, there would be one perpetual quarrel between our souls and God. God has to be easy to live with, and if He knows you mean right, He will let you make all sorts of mistakes and will not care.

But just as soon as self gets in and you mean wrong, the holiest thing you do is unholy. As soon as you curse your conduct with self or sin, everything you do becomes wrong. But as long as you love God and people, He lets you tumble around a lot and won't mind a bit and sits and watches you as a mother fox, lying in the sunshine with her chin on her paws, with a smile on her face and watches her little puppies. God knows that the most mature of us still need coddling sometimes, and so He is quick to overlook our ignorance, but He is never quick to overlook our sins.

The threatening aspect of our life is sin, and so God is quick to leap on the scene and deal with it. But He never rides us because of formulas we have broken. Therefore, I do not care what anybody says, if I want to pray to the Spirit, I am going to pray to the Spirit. Normally, we do not, but if we want to, let us do it and smile and say, "If I'm making a mistake, God understands." He knows we mean the whole Godhead. When I say, "Our Father which art in heaven, Hallowed be thy name" (Matt. 6:9), I mean all the persons in the Trinity.

How important are our formulas in the light of sin, death and the judgment? How important is it that we hear these simple words? Have you noticed that when our Lord Jesus is talking to the believer and attempting to teach and instruct the believer's heart, He gets so profound sometimes that you have to keep your chin up to keep from drowning from the glory of it? But when He tells us how to get saved, He makes it so simple, so very simple. "Verily, verily, I say unto you, He that heareth my word, and believeth on him that sent me, hath everlasting life, and shall not come into condemnation; but is passed from death unto life" (John 5:24).

Those words are so simple that nobody will believe it. It is as though if someone would find an elixir of life or a universal panacea for the cure of all diseases, nobody would believe it at first, and everybody would say it could not be so. Jesus Christ our Lord has laid down here a universal panacea. He has given us the true elixir. He has told us where the fountain of youth is and said it simply consists of hearing the words of Jesus and through those words believing on the Father who sent Jesus. And if we do that we have everlasting life and we shall not come into condemnation but have passed from death to life.

Discipline, Not Condemnation

What happens to the Christian who breaks down, who sins? The answer is the difference between coming into discipline and coming into condemnation. The believer who fails his God and sins comes into discipline but not into condemnation. The sinner is already under condemnation.

Let me illustrate what I mean. There were two men, Simon Peter and Judas Iscariot. Peter heard Jesus Christ and believed on the Father and passed into life and was out of condemnation. In a desperate moment, he made a mistake and failed God. Judas Iscariot also made a mistake and failed God.

Christ looked on Peter, brought him under discipline and he wept copiously, as it says in the original, tears and floods of tears he wept copiously (see Luke 22:61-62). In his repentance, he was restored to favor and blessing (see John 21:15-19). Although he did come under discipline, he did not come into condemnation.

Judas Iscariot was a different story. He went out, and the Scriptures tell us that as the son of perdition he went to his own place (see Acts 1:25). Judas Iscariot never believed on the Father or the Son and was never regenerated, and he went out into condemnation. Peter who believed but failed went out to discipline and forgiveness.

There is the difference. You come to Jesus Christ as you are, weary and worn and sad. Come to Jesus Christ as you are, sinful and tired and without self-confidence, knowing that you cannot live it, and knowing that, you come anyway. Hear the words of Jesus and believe on the Father and the Son. Trust the words of Jesus, that is, believe on Him, and God will give you eternal life and promise you that you will never come into judgment or condemnation.

God has given me a passage of Scripture to which I claim and hold tight even though I do not fully understand it. "For this is as the waters of Noah unto me: for as I have sworn that the waters of Noah should no more go over the earth; so have I sworn that I would not be wroth with thee, nor rebuke thee. For the mountains shall depart, and the hills be removed; but my kindness shall not depart from thee, neither shall the covenant of my peace be removed, saith the LORD that hath mercy on thee" (Isa. 54:9-10).

I tell God about this and put my name in here so He will be sure I know who He is talking about: "I'll never be angry again and I'll never rebuke Aiden Wilson Tozer again." Discipline, yes. I expect discipline, but I do not ever expect to see an angry face in God Almighty's heaven again. That is not because I am good, but because He has sent a Redeemer. "In a little wrath I hid my face from thee for a moment; but with everlasting kindness will I have mercy on thee, saith the LORD thy Redeemer" (Isa. 54:8). Because the Lord is our Redeemer, we never need to worry after we have trusted Him, if we do trust and walk on with Him.

10

The Eternal Christ Is Both Judge and Savior

*For as the Father hath life in himself; so hath he given to the
Son to have life in himself; And hath given him authority to
execute judgment also, because he is the Son of man.*

JOHN 5:22-29

It is only because of the Incarnation that God in His wisdom
and grace can bring all of humanity to a point of accountability.
This is something we can both rejoice over and be fearful of,
and it enables God to bring all of humanity to His judgment bar.

No matter where you go in the world, you will run into the
concept of judgment, with variations in detail. The basic concept of judgment is simply that human beings are morally accountable. The basis of this accountability is the fact that we
have life derived from another and not from ourselves. Because
our life has come from another, we have a moral responsibility
to that one who gave us life. The Father, so the Scriptures teach
us, has life in Himself; therefore, nobody can judge the father.

God is not a derived; He is the original. Furthermore, the Scripture says, "For as the Father hath life in himself; so hath he given to the Son to have life in himself" (John 5:26), so no one can judge the Son. The Son is of the Father alone. Out of this comes the concept of universal judgment. While we are free to make moral choices, we are nevertheless under necessity to account for some authority for those choices.

I have used a word and a phrase—"free" and "under necessity"—and one seems to cancel the other out. But there is nothing inconsistent here. Men are free to decide their own moral choices, but they are also under the necessity to account to God for those choices. That makes them both free and bound, for they are bound to come to judgment and to give account for the deeds done in the body.

In Ralph Waldo Emerson's famous essay, he develops the idea that there is no such thing as a future judgment. Everything is judged and sentenced and rewarded or punished now. To illustrate this, he said, "The thief only steals from himself." This of course is not the universal belief, and it is not the belief of the Old Testament, nor is it the teaching of the New Testament, nor the teaching of the Church. It was hatched out of the head of the great man who lived in Concord, Massachusetts.

Inadequate Concepts of Judgment

As anyone might expect, there are many wrong and inadequate concepts of judgment. Again, wherever you have two or three gathered together you will have at least two or three concepts of judgment. It is like the Old Testament Scripture that said, "Every man did that which was right in his own eyes" (Judg.

17:6). Let me name a few concepts of judgment that are popular but inadequate.

The first concept is *the operation of the law of compensation*. I take something out of my left pocket and I put it in my right pocket. Everything you do in one direction has to be counterbalanced by something in the opposite direction.

Another inadequate concept of judgment is that *we are accountable only to society*. Certainly, there is a world of truth in this, but it's only part truth. When we do something against society, we are accountable to society. But we are also responsible to God and accountable to Him for our actions. Much of this has to do with public opinion. Public opinion is what judges you and indeed has already judged the things you do. Proof of what I'm saying was brought home to me a few years ago.

I was walking down the street when a little boy took a good look at me as I walked along. Usually I am friendly to children, but I was preoccupied that day, and when I got within hearing distance of him, he looked up at me and said, "Hello, pickle puss." He had me figured out already. I was a pickle puss, and I was responsible to human society for the very shape my face was in. I was not mad at anybody, but he evidently thought I was not as cheerful looking as I might have been. He thought he would needle me a little, which he did. So we are responsible to society for everything we do.

There are many ways in which we are accountable to public opinion. Simply driving down the highway causes people to conclude that you are either a good driver and a good person or you are a road hog—one or the other. Your neighbors will judge you as a good neighbor or a bad neighbor based on public opinion.

Another inadequate concept of judgment is that *we are accountable to human law*. From the most primitive tribes in New Guinea to the most civilized culture in London or New York or Paris, every nation establishes laws. Those nations expect those laws to be respected and abided by, or suffer the consequences.

Somebody may point out the lawbreaker. Here is a person who breaks the law in order to get money. He may rob a bank so that he might get money to pay his taxes or pay something else. But he is keeping one law and breaking another law to get the money to do it. So, the outlaw is an outlaw only in certain details; he keeps the majority of the laws but breaks one law for personal profit or convenience.

An outlaw is never a happy man because he is accountable to the law even while he is breaking it, and he is miserable even while he is flaunting the law.

There is another inadequate concept of judgment, and that is that *man's accountability is to himself alone*. According to this concept, each and every person stands before the bar of his own reason and of his own conscience, which would be the judge and jury.

The basis of this is the idea of relativity of morals and is being taught in many of our universities today. Simply put, it is that each man is a law unto himself. Nothing is really bad or good. Good is whatever brings social approval, and bad is whatever brings social disapproval. Something may be good today and tomorrow it might be evil.

This is probably the worst concept of judgment in all of society. Because if it is true, then there would be as many moral codes as there are human beings, and each would be his own witness, prosecutor, judge, jury and jailer. That is so silly it is scarcely worth any consideration.

I never underestimate the ability of man to get things mixed up. Anyone with an eloquent manner can convince people to believe anything. This of course is the core of all the cults that have sprung up throughout the years.

Let me ask this question. How can a man be accountable to himself? If this is true, then how does it play out?

Someone might say, "He's accountable to his conscience." And I can see the argument here. But then my question is, to whom is his conscience accountable? How in the world can I be my own prosecutor, my own witness on the prosecuting side, my own prosecuting attorney, my own judge, my own jailer and my own executioner? I know it sounds quite learned and mystical and very poetic and dreamy, but when you consider it, it is simply ridiculous. It is an absolutely inadequate concept of judgment, for I never knew anybody to be hard on himself—to stand as judge and jury of himself and punish himself. Most people are very easy on themselves.

I know if I were to be my judge, jury, prosecutor and executioner, I think I would lose my axe. I certainly would not cut off my own head. I would not have the courage to do it.

Accountable to God

Understanding God as He is revealed in the Scriptures, it is quite clear that He is not going to make men ultimately accountable to self. And to take this further, neither is he going to make you and me ultimately accountable to the law or human society. We are accountable finally, and ultimately, to the

One who gave us life. We are accountable to God alone. I believe it is the absence of this that makes soft, spineless Christians and churches without any meaning in them at all.

The simple truth is, society cannot reach us in that sphere of our being where we are most vitally accountable to God and to ourselves.

As a human being and an American, I am accountable to public opinion, and I am accountable to the law of the land. But I am also accountable to myself and to my God; and human society cannot touch me there. The laws of the land and public opinion only go so far. There is truth in them, but not the entire truth. There is something beyond all of this.

Take for example a man who commits suicide. Say he takes a gun, turns the gun on his head and blows out his brains. At that point he is not accountable to public opinion or to the law of the land. He is gone beyond that and he now is accountable to a higher authority, because once he dies, the society cannot punish him.

There are many things society and the law of the land cannot deal with. Jesus understood this when He said, "Ye have heard that it was said by them of old time, Thou shalt not commit adultery: But I say unto you, That whosoever looketh on a woman to lust after her hath committed adultery with her already in his heart" (Matt. 5:27-28). The Jewish law could deal with adultery, but when it came to lust of the heart, the law could not touch it.

This kind of nonsense has even invaded our churches. Whenever a church backslides from the truth and runs away from the plain Word of God, that church begins establishing its own laws. One church I heard of, that once was a solid Bible-preaching church, advertised that on a certain Sunday morning the topic of the good Reverend's sermon was going to be on peptic ulcers. Now, what that has to do with the Bible and going on with God baffles my imagination. If I hung around that congregation for long, I probably would develop a peptic ulcer myself.

It is amazing what depths we fall to and what fools we become when we become a law unto ourselves.

In the city of Detroit some years ago, the sign out front of a church announced that next Sunday morning at 10:45 A.M., the Reverend Doctor would preach on the theme, "Who Killed Cock Robin." How the good Reverend knew who the culprit was is anybody's guess.

An anonymous ancient proverb says, "Those whom the gods wish to destroy they first make mad." The judgment of God will begin to fall on the church. When they cease to believe in the judgment of God, you never know what that church will get into next or where it will go. It was belief in the accountability of man to his Maker that made America great at one time.

One of the great leaders of America was Daniel Webster. That great bulging brow of his and those blazing eyes used to hold the Senate spellbound as he stood there and talked to them not with silly quips or funny remarks. The Senate in those days was not composed of half-baked comedians but of strong, noble statesmen who carried the weight of the nation on their shoulders.

Someone said, "Mr. Webster, what do you consider the most serious thought that has ever entered your mind?" He said, "The most solemn thought that has ever entered my mind is the accountability to my Maker." Men who talked like that could not be corrupted and bought off. And they would not have to be ashamed to have their telephone calls read back to them. They were not worried about what people thought so much as the fact that they were accountable to God.

Our Righteous Judge

In order for someone to judge humanity certain criteria need to be put in place. Not just anybody can do this. Along with this, he must have authority to execute the judgment that is needed. Another criterion would be that the ones being so judged must be accountable to the judge. Some kind of relationship needs to be established.

Out in the world, a group of men may establish a law, as in our country over 200 years ago. People are being judged today based upon the laws established then, but not really knowing the people who established those laws. This is not the way it is in the kingdom of God. To be a judge, according to the Scripture, the judge judges those who are accountable to Him. Accountable not only by law imposed by another, but accountable morally and vitally rather than merely legally. In order to be a righteous judge of mankind, the judge has to have a variety of qualities or attributes.

All-knowing

The judge that we have to do with has all knowledge. He is all knowing without any exception. In order for this judge to judge rightly, there is no room for error. In our judicial system, many judges have made errors because they did not have all the facts before them. Human justice does its best, but because it is not all wise, it makes mistakes. There are some in prison today who are serving lifetime sentences that because of a mistake are in prison.

But when we come to God Almighty, He is never going to judge anybody with only partial information. God does not make mistakes; neither does He allow any error or lack of information come into the situation. This judge that judges us must be one who has all wisdom; therefore, we must eliminate Paul the apostle, Moses the lawgiver and even Elijah. These were good men but they were men only and had only finite knowledge and wisdom. The God who judges us is the judge who has infinite wisdom and is all knowing.

When it comes to judging a soul that will live for all eternity, there is no room allowed for mistakes. The judge of humanity is going to have to be one that will never need the testimony of a third party. Today they bring witnesses in and the judge sits solemnly and listens to the testimony. The witness says, "I saw him do this, I heard him say that," and if the witness is lying, the judge is misled. But the judge of mankind is not dependent upon the testimony of another.

Christ says, "I can of mine own self do nothing: as I hear, I judge: and my judgment is just; because I seek not mine own will, but the will of the Father which hath sent me" (John 5:30).

The basic criterion to judge all of humanity is perfect and complete knowledge.

Impartial

Another criterion plays into this. The judge must be absolutely impartial and disinterested, without any personal interest in the case whatsoever.

Many a judge has been severe in judgments because election time was coming up or because public opinion was getting strong. The newspapers were getting on him, and to save his political career, he passed a severe sentence or did not pass a sentence. His motives were ulterior and false. The Son of God says that His judgment is just because He does not seek His own will, but the will of the Father. Christ can be the judge because He is personally related and yet disinterested, with nothing to gain or lose by His judgment. But all the glory belongs to God.

Empathetic

Another important criterion to qualify the judge is a sympathetic understanding. Personally, I do not want to be judged by some archangel that never shed a tear. Nor do I want to be judged by a seraphim that never felt pain. I do not want to be judged by a cherub that never knew human grief or disappointment or woe.

For the judge to be the judge of humanity, He must be one of them. Jesus said, the Father hath given the Son power to execute judgment because He is a Son of man. Because He is a Son of man, He not only can be their advocate above, the Savior by the throne of love, but He can also be their judge to sit upon the throne.

With that in place, it eliminates all false accusations. Then there will be no dodging, no whimpering, no whining, no crying on our wrists and saying, "But Lord, You didn't understand." He does understand, because He became one of us and walked among us. Never was a tear He did not share; never a bitter disappointment He did not feel; never a grief He did not suffer;

never a temptation that did not come to Him; never a critical situation that He was not in.

This brings us to the ultimate judge of all humanity, the one who alone qualifies, and none other. This one is Jesus Christ. Because He is the Son of man, He has authority to execute judgment. Christ qualifies on every count to be the judge of humanity. The tears that He shed, the pains that He suffered and the grief He bore made Him not only a just but a sympathetic judge of humanity. Now His presence in the human race is our present judgment on sin.

"And Jesus said, For judgment I am come into this world, that they which see not might see; and that they which see might be made blind" (John 9:39).

Both Savior and Judge

This represents one Bible doctrine grossly misunderstood. There are many doctrines, important doctrines, neglected by the Bible teachers of today. This would be one of those doctrines: Jesus Christ is the judge of mankind, but the Father judges no man. "When the Son of man shall come in his glory, and all the holy angels with him, then shall he sit upon the throne of his glory: And before him shall be gathered all nations: and he shall separate them one from another, as a shepherd divideth his sheep from the goats" (Matt. 25:31-32).

It is He who is the judge, and when the judge of humanity shall appear, He will have the shoulders of a man and the face of a man, the man Christ Jesus. God has given Him authority to judge mankind so that He is both the judge and the Savior of man. That makes me both love Him and fear Him; love Him because He is my Savior, and fear Him because He is my judge.

Unfortunately, the ten-cent-store Jesus being preached now by many men is not the Jesus that will come to judge the world. This plastic, painted Christ who has no spine and no justice, but is a soft and pliant friend to everybody, if He is the only Christ, then we might as well close our books, bar our doors and make a bakery or garage out of our church buildings.

The popular Christ being preached now is not the Christ of God nor the Christ of the Bible nor the Christ we must deal with finally. For the Christ that we deal with has eyes as a flame of fire. And His feet are like burnished brass; and out of His mouth cometh a sharp two-edged sword (see Rev. 1:14-16). He will be the judge of humanity. You can leave your loved ones in His hands knowing that He Himself suffered, knowing that He knows all, no mistakes can be made, there can be no miscarriage of justice, because He knows all that can be known.

It was said one time as an afterthought that Jesus need not that any should testify of man, for He knew what was in man. "Marvel not at this: for the hour is coming, in the which all that are in the graves shall hear his voice, And shall come forth; they that have done good, unto the resurrection of life; and they that have done evil, unto the resurrection of damnation" (John 5:28-29).

This coming out of the grave will be at the invitation of the Son of God Himself. Like an army file officer, He will command and they will stand on their feet, a great army to receive judgment, and the judgment will be based strangely enough upon the kind of life they lived in this world. That is another forgotten doctrine, but it is here. They that have done good, unto the resurrection of life; they that have done evil, unto the resurrection of damnation. And this is the judge of all.

Jesus Christ our Lord, the judge with the flaming eyes, is the one with whom we must deal. We cannot escape it. They can shrug Him off and drive away in a cloud of fumes, but everyone must come back and deal with Him finally. Be sure of one thing, He will either be Savior now or judge then. And the tenderness and sympathy of the Savior now will be laid aside while the justice and severity of the judge comes to the front. Without canceling out one, He will exercise both. So that Jesus Christ is both the Lord and the judge of men as well as the Savior of men.

Isaac Watts, in his hymn "Not All the Blood of Beasts," illustrates this very truth:

Not all the blood of beasts
On Jewish altars slain
Could give the guilty conscience peace
Or wash away the stain.

But Christ, the heav'nly Lamb,
Takes all our sins away;
A sacrifice of nobler name
And richer blood than they.

My faith would lay her hand
On that dear head of Thine,
While, like a penitent, I stand,
And there confess my sin.

My soul looks back to see
The burdens Thou didst bear
When hanging on the cursed tree,
And knows her guilt was there.

Believing, we rejoice
To see the curse remove;
We bless the Lamb with cheerful voice,
And sing his bleeding love.

In the Old Testament, the sinner would come to the priest and say, "I have sinned and I bring a lamb," or some other offering. They would take that creature and the sinner would lay his hand on the head of the beast and they would kill it and sprinkle its blood; and the sin that he had committed would be forgiven him.

Those of you who do not want Jesus as a judge, you had better think seriously now about Him as a Savior and stand like a penitent or kneel like one and confess your sin. "My soul looks back to see the burdens thou didst bare when hanging on the cursed tree and knows her guilt was there." Do you believe that your guilt was there in that cursed tree? He that knew no sin became sin for us that we might become the righteousness of God in Him (see 2 Cor. 5:21), and then Watts's hymn says, "Believing, we rejoice to see the curse remove" (see Gal. 3:13-14).

I have seen this song edited and twisted around; some educated, sophisticated editor who did not like this word "curse" removed it. He fixed it up, but I will not sing it. I sing this one: "Believing, we rejoice to see the curse remove." What curse? The curse of the broken law. The curse of sin. "We bless the Lamb with cheerful voice and sing His bleeding love." How wonderful all this is! What a wonderful song of triumph! What a song full of theology and meaning and gospel. What the blood of goats could not do, the blood of Christ is doing and has done.

Which is He going to be for you: Savior or Judge? He will be one or the other. If He is the first, He will not be the second. But if He is not the Savior, He will be the Judge. I, for my part, cannot afford to face Him as my Judge. I must have His protecting blood and face Him as my Savior now. He knows too much about me for me to brazenly barge into His presence and let Him judge me.

The Scriptures tell us of certain ones that have sent their sins on before the judgment. You can send your sins on before the judgment, having judged, settled and dispelled them now while you are still on the earth. The Savior will cover your sins. As the old brother said, "If Jesus Christ had covered our sins with His life when they took His life away, they had been exposed but He covered them with His death. And by His death forever, He put my sins where they cannot be found, for the blood of the everlasting covenant."

Look back and see the burden Jesus bore, lay your hand of faith on His holy head and confess your sins, and the curse will be removed and you can say, believing, I rejoice to see the curse removed. "We bless the Lamb with cheerful voice and sing his bleeding love."

11

The Wonder
and Mystery of
the Eternal
Christ Identifying
with Man

And a great multitude followed him, because they saw his miracles
which he did on them that were diseased.

John 6:1-13

Whenever you see Jesus in the Gospels, He is usually surrounded by people. There was that one exception, when He
withdrew and went with His disciples to a mountain. This was
typical of the One who came to walk among men to be the
Savior of humanity.

We take so many things for granted in the Bible and do not
take the time to inquire about them. And we fail to acquire the
help that it would give us if we would ask the question, "Why
was He constantly with the people?" The question becomes

more vivid when we notice that all logic is against Him being with them.

Notice who He was and who they were and you will see that logic and common reason, expectation based upon reason, would be over on the other side. For this was Jesus whom John so carefully pictured for us in his first chapter as being the "Word made flesh." Before the beginning and in the beginning He was God, and still is God; and from eternity He had gazed on God and He Himself had received the worship of the heavenly powers.

I do not claim to know much about the heavenly powers. Today I am a greater believer in the existence of beings other than us than I was 20 years ago—creatures that are presently superior to us in rank and degree. I think it is quite proper that we should so conclude, because if it is true, and I think it is true, then earth is a reflection of heaven. Henry Drummond, in his great book *Natural Law and the Spiritual World,* said that the spiritual world was the natural world extended infinitely upward.

Personally, I do not believe he was totally correct in his assumption. I think he is accurate except that he has it upside down. I believe that the natural world is the spiritual world projected down. Earth is the shadow of heaven, and if we knew more about earth, we would know more about heaven. The same God made both, and while sin has entered and marred and polluted the earth in all of its ways, there still remain yet some similarities. The same laws that rule above, rule below in nature, and everywhere else except in the rebellious heart of man. So God made the creatures below in various orders. We read in the Bible how He did it, and the most casual student of nature will note that the creatures down here are graded upward. Begin with the angleworm burrowing in the earth, helping the farmer, unknown to him, to make his ground mellow and the loam soft. And the angleworm on up flies the birds and then walks the great mean beasts, and finally there is man.

If order follows order upward in the scale of light here below in this backyard of God, then why are we to doubt that in the front yard of God, in His heavens, it should not be pretty much the same? Why should we doubt if there are gradations of beings in heaven, if there are watchers and the holy ones, if there are principalities and powers and mights and dominions? If there are angels and archangels, if there are seraphim, cherubim, strange beasts and living creatures, why should we doubt it? Why should we not accept it as not only a matter of faith but also as a matter of common reason that the same God who made the heavens above made the earth beneath?

I delight in the fact that God is an artist, and the handiwork and the fingers of God are upon everything He does. No artist can escape himself. He has his own style; and though he says, "I'll be different this time; I'm going to get clear out of my skin," the fellow that knows the artist well finds his skin. You cannot escape your own personality. You cannot escape your own genes; and when God made the heavens, He made the earth, and the same mark of God is on the earth that is in the heavens above. The God who made the world above made the world below; and though sin has entered and man fell and the shadow fell over the earth, there is still similarity, there are still some of the fingerprints of God all over His wonderful world.

The great state of Pennsylvania, where I was born, is the most beautiful state in the United States, the most beautiful part of the world. Valleys, rolling hills and flowing rivers, and in the morning, a fog like great lovely ribbon hanging above the river, disappearing into the sky later on when the sun comes up. All that beauty, and it has God's hand upon it. The only marks of ugliness are man's marks, for man has taken his great bulldozers and gone halfway up the hill and done what they call strip mining.

These great bulldozers have dug the top of the earth off until they have come to coal. To get a little cheap coal they have marred and chewed up the lovely face of nature. It will take a generation to bring the beauty back into the hillsides of Pennsylvania. Some of those hills are marred where greedy men have gone in and marred the face of God's lovely world for the sake of getting a few extra dollars.

God has made it all, and so it is all lovely in its time; and the God who made the earth also made the heavens above. So I say again, I believe there are orders of heaven above and that God made those heavens. He made them very much the way He made the earth, only pure in spirit in place of material. And when you and I get there, we are going to feel very much at home.

Our Lord had been there from ancient time. How long had He been there? He had been there since before they were. For He was in the beginning with God, and it was His voice that called out of the vacuity of nothingness all that loveliness above yonder. Before there were any hills or valleys, He was. And before there were any archangels or seraphim, He was. Before principalities and powers and mights and dominions raised their scepters, He was. This was the One who now is among the people, and He had received the worship of these heavenly powers. They had knelt unto Him and cried, "Holy, holy, holy is the Lord God Almighty," and they had come in great crowds, knelt at His feet and rendered homage to Him, the Son of the Father everlasting. He had heard the voice of God and had gazed upon all the moral beauty that is in heaven.

I think the voice of God must be very wonderfully musical. This voice of God had sounded in the ears of the Son of God from before the beginning times when as yet there was no creation. He had heard all this, He had seen all this, He had filled His eyes with the beauty of it all and He had heard the chant of the creatures crying, "Holy, holy, holy is the Lord God of hosts." And He Himself was the unspeakably holy one.

If I had the voice of Demosthenes or the descriptive power of Shakespeare or the terrible, incisive language of the apostle Paul, I could not overstate my case in attempting to describe who He was and is. Attempting to describe His impeccable holiness, His unsullied righteousness, His utterly unapproachable, wondrous, glorious person. This was the One who had walked among the holy creatures and had gone from watcher to holy one and had heard watchmen crying, "Watchmen, what of the night?"

Where Is God?

Now we find Him walking among the people. And who are these people?

Scriptures describe them long ago when God saw that the wickedness of man was great in the earth and every imagination of the thoughts of his heart was only evil continually. That is what it says in Genesis 6:5, and if I want to read from the first chapter of Romans, I could carry that on a bit and show you what God says about people. The Word of God does not have any good thing to say about people. Even when you grudgingly admit that a man does something that is not bad, it says, "If ye then, being evil, know how to give good gifts unto your children, how much more shall your Father which is in heaven give good things to them that ask him?" (Matt. 7:11).

God never forgets that the imagination and thoughts of a man's heart is only evil continually. Let us not imagine that those among whom Jesus walked were the lovely creatures that men have painted on canvases. Let us not think that all the children had shiny faces, all the women were beautiful and all the men strong, noble and square-shouldered. Let us see them for what they were. Let us be realistic and remember that they were capable of every sin under the sun.

Let us remember that they were filled with every kind of iniquity and their sin and wickedness were great in the earth, and every imagination of their thoughts and of their hearts was only evil continually. And He who had never had an evil thought was among men who had never had a holy thought. He who had never gazed upon anything but moral beauty was among men who had never gazed upon anything but moral ugliness. Think of how it was to be with those who worshiped God in reverence and then be among those who worshiped themselves and the goods of this world and all the false gods the world has taken for her own.

All logic was against that. Why? The first judgment is, He could not stand these people; this Holy One could not stand these unholy ones. And the offense against His holiness must be too great. Reason has a strong case in a philosophy called deism. And the doctrine of deism simply carries my argument on to its logical conclusion and says it cannot be.

A Philosophy Called Deism

Long before seventeenth-century deism was ever born, there had been those called Gnostics, against whom Paul aimed his terrible barrages. Those Gnostics said it was impossible that God should ever touch man. It was impossible that God should ever touch matter. It was unthinkable and blasphemous that you should ever say God created anything. God never created anything. God is too holy to touch matter. God could not possibly touch matter. Matter was created by demiurges (a deity in Gnosticism, Manichaeism and other religions that creates the material world and is often viewed as the originator of evil) and demigods that God had thrown out from Himself in waves. God Himself would never stoop to lay His unspeakably holy hands upon unholy matter.

When we come to the seventeenth century and over into the eighteenth century, we have such men as Herbert Spencer, and the doctrines were the same. He said, "Doctors are gods, nobody doubts there's a god."

Men say that Voltaire was an atheist. Voltaire was no more an atheist than I am a Buddhist. Voltaire was a deist. He believed that God existed, and when some priest said an unpleasant thing about him because of his so-called atheism, Voltaire turned on him and said, "I've said more good things about God than you ever did." I am not sure but that he was right.

This is the difference between an atheist and a deist: "A" meaning "not," and "theo" meaning god, and "eist" is somebody that builds beliefs. Therefore, we have an atheist who is somebody who says there is no God. That is simple enough. Then we come to the word "agnostic." An agnostic is one that says, "I don't know whether there is a God or not." Then we have a deist; and that is what Spencer was and what Tom Paine was and the rest of the atheists of the seventeenth and eighteenth centuries. They were not really atheists, they were deists, yet men called them atheists.

What does a deist say? A deist says, "Yes, there's a God. There must be a God." Voltaire once took his watch from his pocket and said, "You might as well tell me that that watch made itself as to tell me that this vast internal locking system made itself. There is a God." He was hard on the priests and hard on hypocrites, but he was a deist. The deists say that God never got close to humanity. How could it be? "Why the great eternal God that made the heaven and earth is too exalted, too high up, too transcending ever to think that He'd be interested in you or me." That is deism.

Theism (for Lack of a Better Word)

What are we then? We are theists. The word is from the Greek and the Latin and was given to unbelievers. It is a nice trick if you can get away with it, but you and I are theists.

Now, a deist is one who believes in God but does not believe God cares anything about us. Therefore, there is no Savior and no Bible. A theist is one who believes there is a God and that God does care something about us; there is a Savior, and there is a Bible.

Down in the South, some politician with a little education was running against another man and he knew some of the voters in the mountains were not so much up on definitions. So he started a rumor that his opponent had been celibate up until the time he was married; he had been guilty of celibacy. And the people said, "Why, I never thought or dreamed of such a thing. That man was guilty of celibacy before he was married. We won't vote for him." He swept an easy victory because this other man had been single up to the time he was married.

Logic says that God could not have been among them. Logic says, being who He was and they being what they were, He could not have been among them. Strong reason argues that He could not have been among us. It could not be that the Lord of glory should come down to the men of low earth—that He who walks among the interstellar spaces should come down, confine Himself and be among men. Why did He come?

God with Us

The Bible says that He was here among people; and if you read the Gospels, you will find that He was there all right. He was there sleeping among them, eating with them, sitting down, going to their funerals, going to their weddings, patting their babies on the head, helping them up on their feet when they fell. He was among them, and He was God. Now, why was He among them?

He was there by the awful mystery of the Incarnation. All that God is had become all that man is, except sin. Keep that in mind. And when He became incarnated, He was irrevocably committed to the human race.

When our Lord Jesus Christ came to the womb of the Virgin Mary, He came to the point of no return. He committed Himself irrevocably while the ages roll and beat themselves to nothingness, while world spins after world and millennium follows millennium, He will be what He was. All that God was became all that man is, except sin, and there is no return for Him. He came to share man's grief; He came to share their pains; He came to share and bear their sins, vicariously, for He Himself never sinned. If He had, He could not have borne ours.

Years ago, I ran into a passage in Psalm 69 that I could not understand. I knew this psalm was what the scholars call a messianic psalm. It was a prophecy of Jesus, and it was a prayer of Jesus. In this psalm, we come to this passage: "Thou knowest my foolishness; and my sins are not hid from thee" (v. 5). And I said to myself, "Now there is confusion somewhere; if Jesus Christ never sinned, according to the New Testament, then how could He pray, 'Thou knowest my foolishness; and my sins are not hid from thee' in the Old Testament?" Then the answer moved in over my heart and it has satisfied it ever since. That is, when the Bible says He never sinned, it means He never personally sinned; but when He prayed to God, "Thou knowest my sin," He was talking about vicarious sin—the sin He had taken upon Himself and made His own.

The critics of vicarious atonement have a lot in their favor. When they argue, "I can't see this Jesus dying for you. I can't see this transfer of responsibility from one personality to another." And by illustration they say, "How would it be if a man were brought up before a court of law and charged with murder, and he was found guilty of murder, and the judge said, 'Stand,' and he stood, and the judge said, 'Do you have anything to say before sentence is passed upon you?'

"And he said, 'Nothing, your honor.'

"Then the judge said, 'You have been found guilty after due process of the law and after a fair and just trial. A jury of your peers unanimously has decided that you committed premeditated murder; the laws of the state under which you live require that you die; therefore, I sentence that man over there to hang by the neck until death.'"

A man over here commits the murder, but the judge sentences a man over there to die for it. How do you get that way? Where is there any justice in heaven? Therefore, they throw out the whole idea of vicarious atonement, saying it cannot be. Moral responsibility cannot be transferred from one personality to another personality.

The strange part about it is they are right. Evangelists and preachers have taken theology and popularized it and have made horrifically complicated what was very simple. The simple fact is there never was made a transfer of moral responsibility from one personality to another in atonement. But in Jesus Christ Himself, we became part of Him and He became part of us and took us up into Himself so that in one sense, when He died, as Paul said, we all died. Instead of the law putting one man to death for all, He put all men to death and raised from the dead all who believe in Jesus Christ, so that every man dies for his sins. The sinner dies alone and the Christian dies in Christ. But every man dies for his sins. He either dies by joining his heart to Jesus Christ, and is tucked up under the wings of Jesus and dies in the body of Christ, or else he dies alone in his sins.

Jesus used those terrible words, "Ye shall die in your sins" (John 8:24). What language can we borrow that could describe anything more utterly shocking and horrible than to say he died in his sins? The dog dies in his vomit and the pig in her wallow and the man in his sin.

The Christian dies too. It says we were crucified with Christ. Have you noticed that? Christ the Head gathered us all up into Himself and died as we died, and because He was God, His death for us could mean atonement and resurrection. If we had died alone and in ourselves there would have been no resurrection into eternal life. But because we died in Him and with Him, there is a resurrection unto eternal life and the new birth and glory to come.

He was here, this Jesus, and all that was God had become all that was man, except sin. And He had gathered us up into Himself. The old Athanasian Creed explains it very carefully: "Although he is God and human, yet Christ is not two, but one. He is one, however, not by his divinity being turned into flesh, but by God's taking humanity to himself. He is one, certainly not by the blending of his essence, but by the unity of his person. For just as one human is both rational soul and flesh, so too the one Christ is both God and human."

The churches believed that all down the centuries. But the Incarnation was not a degradation. A man once attempted to explain the Incarnation by saying, "If you could imagine an archangel coming down to take the body of a toad, it still would not be as ghastly and frightful, as terrible and wonderful, as the incarnation."

Deity did not degrade itself. When Jesus Christ became man, He humbled Himself, but He did not degrade Himself. Deity never degraded itself and never will. When the holy Son of God walked among sinful men, it was no degradation. It was not the body of a toad He inhabited, it was the body of a sinless man, and there was no degradation there. Because He took man up into deity, manhood is to be taken up into God; and if you will read your epistles of Paul, you will find this teaching strong there.

In John 17, you will find Jesus Christ praying that they all may be one as He and the Father are one and teaching the astonishing doctrine that redeemed mankind is to be taken up into God, emotionally at least, and experientially as one with God, as each person of the Trinity are one with each other. I tell you, if the whole Church of Christ could get hold of that idea and meditate on it prayerfully for just a day, it would lift the whole concept of Christianity up into and beyond what it is now.

In the Incarnation, Jesus became all that man is, except sin, and in doing so, He took man up into all that God is, except deity. That is why He was among us. That is why we are theist and not deist. That is why we say there is a God and He is the transcending God, high and lifted up, with His train filling the temple. Logic would say that He could not be among us, but the mystery of the Incarnation says He could be and tells us why.

His Search, Our Rescue

Isaiah 53:5-6 says He took our grief and our pain and our sins, and took our future and our destiny and carries them all in His heart and upon His shoulders, and there was no return from that. He left the earth but He did not leave humanity; He took humanity with Him. He took His humanity with Him into His

183

Godhead, and they are both by the right hand of God. Big brother had come to rescue the little brothers.

Someone once took me to task for saying over the radio that Jesus was our big brother. He said I never ought to talk like that. I did not argue, but I have not quit saying it, because the Bible says that He is the firstborn among many brethren (see Rom. 8:29). And the brethren were lost, and so the firstborn went and found them; or changing the figure, the shepherd was here for His sheep.

Reason says to the shepherd, "Why are you here in the darkness among the bushes? Look at your clothing; it's torn. Why is there a scratch on your cheek, and another on your hand? Why are you here? The night is settling down, there are beasts out here." Logic says, "You should not be here. Back two miles is a cottage. In that cottage are your wife and three children, all waiting for you to come. There's a kettle on the stove, milk in the pail, supper waiting. Why are you here?" And he would say, "Up the hollow somewhere there's a sheep, and that's why I'm here."

It is all the reason I need; all the logic I need. Philosophers say a man belongs back at the house at night. Back where there is a bed and a table and warmth. Logic said God could not be here, but He was. The Shepherd had come for the sheep. Where would the Shepherd find the sheep except where the sheep were? If the sheep could get to Him, He would not have had to come; but because they could not come to Him, He came to them. And the wonder of the Incarnation was more than theological proposition. It was a highly emotional act.

Reason says, "Why should the most holy be among the most sinful? Why should the highest be among the lowest? Why should the God of glory be among men of shame?"

He never answers. He says a sheep is lost up here somewhere, and He is hunting it, that is all. None of the ransomed ever knew how deep was the water He crossed or how dark was the night that the Lord passed through where He found His sheep that was lost. "Out in the desert He heard its cry, sick and helpless and ready to die," so wrote Elizabeth Clephane in the hymn "The Ninety and Nine":

There were ninety and nine that safely lay
In the shelter of the fold,
But one was out on the hills away,
Far off from the gates of gold,
Away from the tender Shepherd's care,
Away from the tender Shepherd's care.

Lord, Thou hast here Thy ninety and nine;
Are they not enough for Thee?
But the Shepherd made answer:
"This of mine has wandered away from Me,
And although the road be rough and steep,
I go to the desert to find My sheep,
I go to the desert to find My sheep."

But none of the ransomed ever knew
How deep were the waters crossed;
Nor how dark was the night

That the Lord passed thro'
Ere He found His sheep that was lost.
Out in the desert He heard its cry,
Sick and helpless, and ready to die,
Sick and helpless, and ready to die.

Lord, whence are those blood drops all the way,
That mark out the mountain's track?
They were shed for one who had gone astray
Ere the Shepherd could bring Him back.
Lord whence are Thy hands so rent and torn?
They're pierced tonight by many a thorn,
They're pierced tonight by many a thorn.

And all thro' the mountains, thunder riv'n,
And up from the rocky steep,
There arose a glad cry to the gate of heav'n,
"Rejoice! I have found my sheep!"
And the angels echoed around the throne,
Rejoice for the Lord brings back His own!
Rejoice for the Lord brings back His own!

12

Living Victoriously in Two Kingdoms

Verily, verily, I say unto you, He that heareth my word,
and believeth on him that sent me, hath everlasting life, and shall not
come into condemnation; but is passed from death unto life.

John 5:24

It is not what a church believes that matters so much as what that church believes enough to emphasize. It is not what a preacher will admit theologically when you pin him down and make him talk; it is what he believes with sufficient urgency to make it a living, constant part of his message.

The problem with much that passes for orthodoxy in this day is not what people believe or even what they do not believe. It is what they believe enough to emphasize. I do not suppose that there is any gospel church but what would say, "We believe that, and we hold that as a part of our creed too." All well and good, but do they believe it enough to lay the emphasis there, to strike it and detonate it and set it off until it explodes into Christian faith and Christian living? That is what matters.

Many churches have not had a conversion since the first Roosevelt was in office, and yet if you were to go to the pastor, deacon or somebody and ask, "Do you believe in the virgin birth?" he would say, "Yes, we sure do."

"Do you believe in the fall of man?"

"Yes, sir."

"Do you believe it's necessary to be born again before we see the kingdom of God?"

"We certainly do."

"Do you believe it is necessary to be justified by faith and made a new creature in Christ Jesus?"

"We certainly do." And they would turn to a book and say, "There it is, that's what we subscribe to."

They believe it, but not strong enough to emphasize it; and the result has been that nobody has entered into it and lived through it. It is not what I hold as a creed that matters so much (although if my creed is wrong, my experience is bound to be wrong too), it is that part of my creed that I have lived through experientially.

Some may wonder why I do not say experimentally. Simply, "experimentally" means in the nature of an experiment, and "experientially" means in the nature of an experience. I am not an experimentalist, in that I do not believe God wants us to experiment with truth. But I am an experientialist in that I believe that everything I hold as true should be mine in living, vibrant experience—what is really mine, that in which I have experience. Not that which I have believed strongly enough to write into a book of creed, but that which I have believed strongly enough to enter into and experience.

That is what is taught here in John 5:24, as well as throughout the whole Bible, and believed by almost all Christians. Yet it is taught so little in our day that it has ceased to have any practical meaning at all to the average rank and file of Bible-believing Christians. It is simply this: There are two worlds that coexist for you and me.

The Coexistence of Two Worlds

God has put us in the middle of two worlds, not the middle of one world, as the materialists believe today, but in the middle of two worlds. God had made us like the animals in our bodies, but He has made us like the angels in our souls. And He has put the two together; because there has been the Fall, sin has come into the world, and man finds that that part of him which is the body, and that part of him which is the soul do not always coincide. Our Lord could say, "The spirit indeed is willing, but the flesh is weak" (Matt. 26:41), so that Paul, in the seventh chapter of Romans could give us the sad picture of the tortured man who wants to go in the right direction but whose physical body will not permit him.

There are two worlds. There is the physical, material world; we have the wind, the sun and the stars at night, and we have the solid earth, which we can jump up and down on and put sidewalks on and build buildings on. We have a material, physical world all around us, and that physical world has gotten into our souls. It is eating its way in. It has conditioned our language. It has given to our language its metaphors and similes and its analogies to a point where our language is of a physical thing.

We say that man is upright, and we think about a tree. We say that it will take a long time, and we think about a journey.

We say that man is low down, and we think in physical terms. We say high society, and we think in terms of elevation. In all our language, we are tied to the earth.

We have made our language fit the crude earth as an old glove fits the hand. For that reason, it takes a little effort of the mind to break out of this physical world in which we live and believe in the coexistence of a spiritual world. I believe there is not only a material world, but there is coexisting with it and impinging upon it a spiritual world. Always remember that which is material is temporal, and that which is spiritual is eternal.

Living in Two Worlds

The New Testament emphasizes the duality of the world in which we live. There is a material world, the first man is of the earth—he is earthly. The second man is the Lord from heaven, and there is your spiritual world. "Except a man be born of water and of the Spirit, he cannot enter into the kingdom of God" (John 3:5). What does that mean? It means that he is in the kingdom of the flesh, and to get into the kingdom of God, you must be born into the kingdom of God.

Yet these two worlds dovetail and coexist, and one is but a shadow of the other. I believe that the material world that you and I know—the "universe," as we call it—is but a shadow thrown down from the throne of God. There is a spiritual world, and you will find that whenever the Scriptures describe heaven or the things of God, it describes them in terms of things of the earth.

Even that mystic Ezekiel, who sat by the river Chebar and dangled his toes in the muddy waters of that foreign river, suddenly saw visions of God, and heaven was opened unto him, and the Word of God came unto him, and the hand of God was upon him. He saw visions indeed of fire coming out of the north, chains of fire unfolding itself, and out of the fire he saw four living creatures come and show that the two worlds, that world of the fire of God's presence and this world in which we live, were very much alike. He began to describe the living creatures and he showed that they were very much like the creatures down here. They were spiritual and eternal and did not partake of a material body, but they had four faces, hands, wings and they traveled on their feet and were describable in material and earthly terms.

That is why I am not a lonely man and why I do not believe any church is any holier than some other place down here on the sidewalk, two blocks away or somewhere else. The kingdom of God coexists with the kingdom of man, and the two are together. One is inward and one is outward. One is internal and one is external. One is of the spirit; the other is of the flesh. One will pass away with a great noise, and the other can never pass away. One is of the earth—it is earthy, and one is of God—it is heavenly.

We think about God as being infinitely removed, on the outer edges of our space. We think of our Lord Jesus Christ as having fled through the corridors of space, and He is now seated at the right hand of God. And all that is true. Certainly, He is seated at the right hand of God as our Advocate forever, our Savior by the throne of grace. But also remember that in the mystery of God's creation and presence the Persons of the Godhead are also with us, and the kingdom of God is close to us. It is not a matter of shouting across the spaces to a God far removed; you can whisper in your spirit to a God that indwells

you if you are a Christian. It does not require sending a tele-
graphic message across the years and spaces to a God far removed;
God can read our heartbeats. Our very mind is frail to God, and
He touches it and knows what we are thinking. This is why we
do not hear much about the coexistence of the two worlds.

Our Lord thought nothing of talking about the children
and their guardian angels that every hour saw the face of "our
Father which art in heaven." And when He was praying and
sweating in the garden before His crucifixion, He could have
had angels. They did come to comfort Him. The angels minis-
ter in love, nothing mysterious about that, nothing strange
about that. But even we evangelicals are such wretched materialists and live for this world so much that the average Christian
knows more about the horsepower of his car and the batting
average of Joe DiMaggio than about the four-faced creatures
that came out of the fire in Ezekiel's vision.

We are materialists in spite of our claim to be spiritual. We
are spiritual in a way, but we certainly think in material terms,
and the whole texture of our brain is material—physical, external,
outward and created. It belongs to the world that perishes, and it
is the work of God by the Holy Ghost and prayer and the Scriptures. It is the work of God to change all the flavor of our being.
It is the work of God to let His water of life flow through the
pores of our spirit until He has washed away all the silt and mud
and clay and dirt, until all the ugly, brackish waters where we
were waterlogged so long in the kingdom of sin are cleansed and
purged and purified; it elevates us and ennobles us until we are
nearer to heaven than we are to earth. It is too bad we have to get
old and gray before we can see this, and yet it is not always so.

A person does not have to be old to be spiritual, and we do not have to live through the decades in order to find this out. It is too bad that it is so for most people. I wonder if it is not because we have assumed that our young people are all about half-cracked and that in religious things they have to be clowned to, played down to, talked down to, teased along, amused and entertained. The result is that for the first years of their life until gray hairs begin to appear, we entertain them, tease them along and amuse them; and then when they get so they do not care for that amusement and entertainment anymore, then we say now they will become saints. I think it is a wretched way to treat young men and women. I do not believe the calendar means anything when it comes to how old a man or woman is.

It is not a question of the passing of years; it is a question of spiritual experience. Young David was so young he did not need to shave. Ruddy-faced and clean, he put to shame his older brothers, and that old King Saul, and the old graybeards in Israel who were afraid. David went out a lad, a spiritual lad, and all through his life he was a spiritual man.

Young Samuel was so young he still had to have a light burning in his room. "I'm afraid, Eli," he would say. Eli would say, "All right," and he would grumble a bit under his breath good-naturedly, get up and light a candle. God Almighty visited him, gave him a vision and prophetic insight and showed him how the whole house of Eli was to be upset; God would raise a new line for the priesthood, and God told this to him when Samuel was only a lad (see 1 Sam. 3).

Christ fed the multitude. And there were two reasons for Him feeding the multitude. One reason was that they were hungry, and He had made them so that they needed food every day. They were hungry, and so the Lord fed them. Now that was the first reason, and you will always find a good salty practicality about everything God does.

When I say there are two worlds, the material and the spiritual, I do not mean to out the material world. God made it also, but not to last. He only made it temporarily, in the same manner as when they put up scaffolding when building a cathedral. The scaffolding is torn down after a while and the cathedral stands for 10 centuries. So God has given us the physical; He is not angry about it, and we do not have to apologize when we touch the physical.

But the woe of the present day is that the physical has swallowed us up and we forget that there is another world. When Jesus fed the multitude, it provided a starting point from which He could elevate their thoughts to consideration of eternal things and could lead them (and us) to the Bread of Life.

They learned very slowly, and our Lord said to them, "Ye seek me, not because ye saw the miracles, but because ye did eat of the loaves, and were filled" (John 6:26). I think I detect a light reproach in His words and a note of sadness there. When He said, "Labor not for the meat that perishes" (v. 27), He said in other words, "You are accepting a deadly philosophy, that there is but one world and that the only thing inside of you that matters is your stomach. If you can keep your stomach comfortably filled, you are well off and you are fulfilling the purpose for which God created you. But this is a deadly philosophy, for you are overlooking the presence of that other world. You have forgotten that there is a spiritual world that flows all around about you as water flows all around the rocks of the bed of the sea."

Their philosophy was a narrow, earthbound thing, and He rebuked them for it and said, "Ye seek me, not because ye saw the miracles, but because ye did eat of the loaves, and were filled. Labour not for the meat which perisheth, but for that meat which endureth unto everlasting life" (John 6:26-27). Still they could not see beyond bread and fish. And they said, "Our fathers did eat manna in the desert; as it is written, He gave them bread from heaven to eat" (v. 31), and they quoted a verse of Scripture.

Then our Lord politely contradicted them, "Moses gave you not that bread from heaven" (v. 32). I want to ask you, how could He say that? When it is written in the Scriptures that He gave them bread from heaven to eat, how could our Lord turn around and say, "Moses gave you not that bread from heaven." In the light of the Hebrew experience, how could He say it?

Anyone, if they had had a scroll of the Scriptures, could have gone back to the story of Israel in the wilderness and how hungry they were and how they cried to God, and God gave them manna. It settled upon them like the dew of night, and it was a small strange thing the size of a coriander seed. It fell like snow upon them; they gathered it up—it was a sort of meal— and they could cook it in half a dozen different ways. It came to them out of heaven, and they said, "This is manna."

"What is it, what is it? Manna." They did not know what it was, and nobody knows what it was to this day. Some unbelieving historian tried to pin it down and said it was the seed of this or that plant. How did it come? It came down just when they needed it and not any other time. How was it that it came down six days a week and did not come down the seventh day?

It was a miracle. They needed bread and God gave them bread. Because it came down, they assumed it came out of the kingdom of love, that it was a spiritual thing. But our Lord said flatly, "Moses gave you not that bread from heaven" (John 6:32). Why was He talking like this to them? He was urging upon them the inadequacy of everything temporal and material.

If I could only make you see the inadequacy of material things, that however good they are, they are not enough. Even though God sends them, still they are not enough.

Religion's External Improvements

We are having an upsurge of religion in the day in which we live; religion is everywhere. You cannot turn the radio on but somebody will be singing about Ezekiel's bone in the middle of a bone. Or they will be singing about, "My, didn't it rain?"

I turn off all those blasphemous noises. I do not listen to them. You can blunder into them, just as if you tramp on a dead cat when you are coming home at night, but you do not stay on it. So when I am turning to find some news or find some decent program, and I run into a bunch of nitwits, faking laughter about a holy thought in the Bible, I do not listen to it. I would just as soon pick up a slimy, maggot-infested dead cat and take it home as I would to listen to, "My, didn't it rain," or, "Bones in the middles of his bones," or whatever they call that blasphemy.

Religion has given us some benefits. Morality for instance.

Improved Morality

If there were more churches, more preachers and more religions there would be fewer crimes and a reduction in juvenile delinquency. It would be safer on the streets. That is all true. And if we step up the percentage number of Christians in Chicago, the danger on dark streets would go down correspondingly. If we could step up numerically the number of converted people in the city of Chicago, our jail cells would be vacant correspondingly. And as the number of good Christians went down numerically, the streets would become more dangerous and the jails more crowded. I believe that with all my heart, so I know that the morality that Christianity brings to the world is a good thing.

But that is not that manna from heaven. That is not that manna that God sent unto the world. That is a temporary thing, a local thing, the thing belonging to Adam's world—this world in which we live—and it will not do you a bit of good five minutes after you are dead.

Improved Culture

I know also the cultural value of religion. You cannot listen to the kind of singing in church and not be culturally better off for it. You cannot sing, "Glorious things of thee are spoken, Zion, city of our God," or, "Break thou the bread of life, dear Lord, to me," or some of the other great hymns of the Church, without having come upon you a sense of appreciation of the sublime and the absolute and the noble. I know the cultural value of religion. Take the average rank-and-file church, whether it is a gospel church or not, and I know the people in it live better than the people that inhabit the saloon downtown.

Here is a modernistic church where the pastor does not believe in very much except ethics and high living; and then down here is the saloon. Nobody has the hiccups in this modernistic church, but they have the hiccups down there in the saloon. They do not carry anybody out of that church, but they carry men out of the saloon. Nobody goes home from that church to beat his wife and fight with his kids, but down in that saloon they do. Any kind of a church, I suppose, is better than a saloon. But the morality and ethics taught by that church is not that manna Jesus spoke of. It is not that true bread from heaven.

Certainly there are many benefits of religion that we love to talk about. The church bell that rings out and says, "Come to the church by the wildwood . . ." All very beautiful, very poetic, and it certainly has had an elevating and ennobling influence in American life. But that is not that true bread from heaven, which my Father giveth unto you. Those are God's gifts and God's benefits, and any kind of goodness is better than the best kind of badness. Any kind of moral standard that is a bit elevated is better than the standard that drags in the dirt. The ethical society that meets down in the Chicago Loop teaching ethics is better off than the halfway house where half-naked women dance to sensuous music.

Then of course, there are the hospitals. They take care of the insane now instead of driving them out into the wilderness. They take care of the blind now instead of having them beg on the street corner. All that is a byproduct of Christianity. And all the good that is being done is a direct byproduct of Christianity.

Those are the byproducts of religion, certainly, but they are not that manna, that true bread, which God gives us.

The Bread of Life that Sustains You

You can begin as low down as possible and go to the heights and enumerate all the benefits of Christianity and all the advantages of the Church, and when you have said it all, our Lord could say, "No, that is not the true bread from heaven." Any person can have all of that, perish and go to hell at last. Jesus said, "I am the bread of life: he that cometh to me shall never hunger; and he that believeth on me shall never thirst" (John 6:35).

Back in the Old Testament there is a strange prophecy, "And in that day seven women shall take hold of one man, saying, We will eat our own bread, and wear our own apparel: only let us be called by thy name, to take away our reproach" (Isa. 4:1).

I do not know whether Christianity today is a fulfillment of that passage or not, but it is an illustration of it. We have everywhere those who call themselves Christian churches. Christian this, Christian that, and they do not want a thing that Jesus has except His name. There is not one thing Jesus has that they want except the external benefits. They want the manna, they want the quail, they want the water out of the rock, they want protection, they want the ethical and moral help He gives. They want to be known as followers of His, because it is popular as long as you do not go too deep. But they do not want His clothes, and they do not want His food. The garments they wear will be strictly garments of their own needlework. And the food they eat will be strictly food of their own supplying. They will not clothe themselves with the robe that is from God, nor do they want to eat that food which God sends down from above to give life unto the world. They only want to take away their pagan reproach by the name of the Man who has earned His right to be respected.

All Christians know better. Whether we do anything about it or not, we know better. "I am the bread of life," he said and "he that cometh to me shall never hunger; and he that believeth on me shall never thirst" (John 6:35).

What eating is to the body, believing is to the soul. I am so afraid that we will think we are saved, and we are not. I am so afraid that somebody got you down some place at an altar, rammed a Christian worker's New Testament up under your nose and showed you by an underlined text that if you came, you would not be cast out and logically forced you to say you were converted. I am afraid of that kind of mechanical religion.

There is such a thing as eating the Bread of Life and knowing you are eating it. There is such a thing as looking in faith to that Bread that cometh down from above and getting it into you and having an inward spiritual religion and knowing for yourself that that which is divine has now come into you. There is such a thing as being assured in your own experience for yourself and not another.

But you say, "I'm saved because the Bible says I'm saved." The Bible does not say you are saved. The Bible lays a condition down whereby you can be saved, but the Bible never tells any individual that he is saved. That cannot be done. God would have to write another Bible to say, "John Jones believeth on me and is therefore saved." God does not write the assurance of your salvation in this book; He tells you how to be saved and then writes the assurance in your heart. If only more evangelical Christians would realize this instead of mechanically stating, "God says I'm saved, and I believe it."

However, if you would say, "God tells me how to get saved, and I've accepted it, and it's real in my life, and I know of a surety that I've passed from death unto life," it would be the difference between the kind of religion we have now and revival. But instead we want to push a button and make it mechanical. If you believe anything, believe John 5:24: "Verily, verily I say unto you, He that heareth my word, and believeth on him that sent me, hath everlasting life, and shall not come into condemnation; but is passed out of death into life."

Now, how do you know that is true of you? It is true of "he that heareth and believeth." But are you that person? How do you know that? John states here for us, "He that believeth on the Son of God hath the witness in himself" (1 John 5:10). I would not give a nickel for the Christian that has no proof of his salvation except he quotes a text. The text will lead you to the fountain, but if you plunge into the fountain and come up wet, I will know you are a Christian. But if you stand on the edge of the water and quote a text, I am not sure. The devil can quote text and is not an unbeliever, do not think he is. The devil believes, all right, and the result is he trembles with fear. But he is not saved and never will be saved.

Many people believe texts, but the text never got inside them. Is Jesus Christ, the Bread of Life, actually inside you? Have you been initiated into that other world, that spiritual world, the kingdom of God? Are you in that kingdom? You can be, because what eating is to the body believing is to the soul.

It will fix your gaze on Him who is the Bread of Life and keep you saying and believing, "Lord, I do believe; I trust Thee; I am now trusting Thee." That which is external will become internal. That which is in the text will get into your heart. That which is in the Bible will get into your soul. You can get up and say, "I know for myself that I know."

13

The Importance of a Proper Concept of God

Believest thou not that I am in the Father, and the Father in me?
The words that I speak unto you I speak not of myself: but the Father that
dwelleth in me, he doeth the works. Believe me that I am in the Father,
and the Father in me: or else believe me for the very works' sake.

JOHN 14:7-11

If we learn anything from history, we learn that no nation has ever risen above the height of its religion. I do not think it would be very difficult to prove this statement. Whether that nation is pure or impure, high or low, depends upon what kind of religion it has.

For a time, a nation can seem to be greater than its religion. It can have a low religion and yet rise to high peaks. But in the qualities that belong to our best humanity, no nation ever yet rose above its religion. I might say that that ought to be a matter of grave concern for the United States of America. If our religion rots, our nation will rot, and there is no law that can be passed, no political party that can come to power, nothing that men can do by way of assuring the nations of the future, that can save us. The nation will only be as great as its religion.

A nation can go below its religion. It can nominally have a high religion yet sink below it just as a man can live at the foot of a mountain and never rise higher than the top of the mountain. All his lifetime he can live below the top of that mountain. Even if he should climb the mountain, he cannot get above the top of it.

A second thing is that no religion ever rose any higher than its concept of God. That is the most vital thing that can be known about any church, any man or any nation. Every religion, whether it is high or low, pure or impure, noble or pagan depends altogether on what it thinks of God.

There have been pagan religions in the past that, while they were pagan and not Christian—they were not redeemed—managed to have a stable society and have some kind of stable pagan worship because they had a lofty concept of God. But no religion can ever go higher than its concept of God. If they have a base God, they will have a base religion. If they have a higher God, they will have a high religion.

I am talking about the religions outside of Christ, the religions that are not Christian. There have been some great religions, but they have all been dependent upon their concept of God. A higher concept of God means that men will strive for higher things and do the best they can even though they are out of Christ and even though they are not born anew. Even though they are not redeemed, they will attempt something better if their concept of God is higher.

One Nation Under God

The most vital fact about any nation is what it thinks of God. I am not a historian, neither by profession nor by any great amount of study. But I do believe I could predict the future of any nation if I could discover exactly what that nation's concept of God is—if I could learn exactly what America thinks of God, what the rank and file, the masses, the lower echelon leadership in America thinks about God; if I could send out a questionnaire and ask the question, "When you think of God, what do you think of? What concept enters your mind when you think about God?"

If I could find an instrument that would tell me what the majority of the people thought about God, I could predict the future of the nation, barring of course the possibility of revival, which would change all that. But even a revival cannot come where a concept of God is low. A missionary cannot go to a heathen land and immediately preach the gospel. One of the first things they have to do is talk about the high God and purge the minds of the people from low and unworthy and ignoble concepts of God. We cannot rise higher than our concept of God.

Personal faith cannot rise higher than a person's concept of God. That is why I for one am indignantly crusading against this concept of God as "the man upstairs." The nice, lovely God that you can slap on the back, laugh, and tell Him a joke; the God that will condescend to anything and pal along with anybody. That kind of God is not the kind of God of the Bible. That is not the God and Father of our Lord Jesus Christ; it is not the God that gave the law to Moses; it is not the God that led the children of Israel out of Egypt; it is not the God of

Isaiah or David, John or Paul; it is not the God of Martin Luther or John Wesley; it is not the God of the Church. It is another kind of God, a soft God that will condescend to anything and overlook anything, with no spine and no character. That God is the divine teddy bear, the huge panda that everybody can cuddle to and coo about but they have no respect for Him because they have no concept of Him.

One Church Under God

I say that not only of a nation but also of a church. You say, "Oh well, every church has the same concept of God, every church knows about God; they read their Bible. They have a Christian concept of God."

Our concept of God could be thought of as a river where we receive tributaries from everywhere—from books and unworthy songs and fiction and religious literature of various kind—until even a church that ought to be a sound, biblical church is a poor, anemic imitation. Our concept of God is likely to be down so that instead of thinking of God as He is—high and lofty, inhabiting eternity, He whose train fills the temple and who walks on the wings of the wind and makes the clouds His chariot—instead of our thinking about that high God, the God we know about or think about or conceive is a very much smaller God.

I believe in evangelism, but I have listened to evangelistic sermons that set forth a God I could not respect and would not want to go to heaven and live with for another few million eternities. I do not want to live with a God like that, the kind of God I have heard set forth in pitiful, nose-wringing, eye-drenching stories as though God were like one of us. The poor little undersized, small-minded preacher gets up and begins to chatter about a God he has made in his own image, and then I'm supposed to want to go to heaven and sit beside the throne of a God I could not respect on earth?

No, I want the God of the Old Testament and the God and Father of the New, or else I do not want to go to heaven. I would rather go somewhere in some neutral place. I have not courage enough to say I would rather go to hell, but maybe a limbo in between where I can stay as far as possible from these teddy bear gods that are being preached now and again.

Some have a lot against John Calvin. I do not go along with everything John Calvin believed, but there is one thing he did believe that I go along with. He had a high concept of God. He believed in God's sovereignty—God high and lifted up. And so do I.

If we could find out exactly what a church thinks about God, we would know that church's future. We would know where they are going for the next several years.

Every Person Under God

The same goes with an individual Christian. Christians go to revival meetings, get on their knees at an altar, beat the bench, pray and imagine they can get an experience that will guarantee them for all time to come. They want something that will give them spiritual security that all will be well, for this world and the world to come.

A man can have an emotional experience at an altar and yet never have any satisfying knowledge of God at all. Never have any high concept of God.

Jesus Christ, our Lord, taught us who God was. Now, this longing after God that Philip revealed here in John 14:8, said, "Shew us the Father." And I am sure he was not a heckler, I am sure he was not a critic. I am sure Philip must have been a good, honest man. I believe he was even a converted man. And Philip was a good-hearted, honest man who honestly wanted to see the Father. The invisibility of the Father had been one of the heavy things he couldn't understand. "Oh God, show us the Father," he said.

An old rabbi was taken in before a king. The king said to him, "You have been talking all over my kingdom about your God, Jehovah. I want to have a showdown here with you. You either produce him or shut up. You let me look at him and see him; if you can produce your God, I will let you preach. But if you can't produce him, you'll have to keep quiet and never mention him again on penalty of death."

The old rabbi said, "Sire, let us walk in the garden." And they walked in the garden. It was a blazing noonday, and the sun was hanging there hot and bright and heavy, and he said, "Sire, behold the sun."

The old king looked at the sun, and then sneezed a couple of times.

The rabbi said, "Sire, look at the sun." He looked again and did the same thing.

Finally, unable to see, he said, "Rabbi, I can't look at the sun."

The rabbi said, "You just said in there, 'Produce God and let me look at him,' and you can't even look at one of the smallest lights that He created. How then can you look at God?"

The old king said, "You win," and walked back into the palace a wiser man.

The invisibility of God has been the string upon which the atheist has harped. We do not have any professional atheists preaching nowadays; we used to have them a few years back, such men as Charles Ingersoll would go up and down the country preaching. One of his favorite tricks was to say that nobody could see God, nobody could produce God; therefore, God was just an idea in people's minds.

I think that Philip, when he said, "Show us the Father," was giving vent to a yearning in his heart. He wanted to get through to God.

He was struggling with the invisibility of God, the fact that God cannot be seen. Close your eyes, pray awhile, open them and see the wall. You act as if God is not visibly there. The effort to know God and find Him and reach Him has been one of the nobler activities of the human race. It has given the world many great religions.

When the apostle Paul came to the streets of Athens and found an altar to the unknown god, he did not sneer; neither did he deliver them a scolding lecture. He said, "The God you're reaching after and can't find is the God I preach." And he began there and took it as a point of departure.

There have been great religions established in an effort to discover God. In addition to great religions, there have been great philosophies, and there are great systems of metaphysics. But God has never been discovered that way because the highest religion outside of Christ is but a man's religion, and the highest philosophy, the highest any man ever climbed on the ladder of philosophy, was a man-made ladder. And no man ever got above his own temple; no man could ever rise above his own brains.

If God could be discovered that way, either by fasting or by visions or by journeys and pilgrimages to Mecca or some river or Palestine; if God could be gotten to that way, and what in us that corresponds to our eyes and our ears and our hands could get to God, then I want to point out something to you. Only the finest minds could know God.

I never could be one of the superior half dozen minds of the world. Would you think that God, the eternal Father, would give redemption to the world and then give it only to a few great minds? Do you think He would send redemption to the world and make it available only to the great scholars? Do you think He would send redemption to the world and let it be available only to those who had unlimited leisure?

American people have more leisure probably than anyone else in the world, because we have so many gadgets to do our work for us. But not even Americans have enough leisure to really be learned in that high, lofty sense of the word. God knew better than that. God was all-wise, and so He brought salvation down.

The message of Christ is not directed to the learned. The man with 15 academic degrees can lay his degrees aside and get on his knees and come like the rest of us. The man of profound learning can come like the rest of us. The man of such leisure that he can travel in Europe and spend winters in Florida and summers in Canada, fishing, he can come the humble way of the rest of us. God sent His message down to the plain people, and that is why I love plain people. I am at home among them. I am one of them, and I love to be among the plain people.

God had to demonstrate Himself some way. He had to satisfy that craving that made Philip say, "Show us the Father." He had to demonstrate Himself to satisfy that cry that David gave: "As for me, I will behold thy face in righteousness: I shall be satisfied, when I awake, with thy likeness" (Ps. 17:15). So what He did was walk to man's level down on earth. Listen, "If ye had known me, ye should have known my Father also; and from henceforth ye know him, and have seen him" (John 14:7).

Here was a Man standing and saying, "If you have become acquainted with me, you already know the Father and you already know what the Father is like." This is the most wonderful thing of all wonders. This is one of the purposes of redemption, and I think the theologians, at least the preachers of theology, are not bearing down hard enough right here. We ought to remember that there is not one purpose in Jesus' incarnation, not two purposes, but multifold purposes in His incarnation.

One of the purposes in His incarnation was that the heart hunger of men and women of the world, those who want to know what God is like, could know what God is like without studying Plato. They can know what God is like without getting academic degrees. They can know what God is like and not have the leisure to read all the learned books of the world. They can know God, because God demonstrated Himself here. Christ is the manifestation of God to men. Christ is God walking among men.

Some theological liberals say that God revealed Himself in Christ. Let us correct their preposition. He did not reveal

Himself "in" Christ, He revealed Himself "as" Christ. There is a change of preposition. Take that "in" out of there. He did not reveal Himself "in" Christ. He did that, but we have not said enough when we say that God revealed Himself "in" Christ. We must go on to say He revealed Himself "as" Christ.

It can be said with certainty that whoever knows Christ knows God. Whoever knows our Lord Jesus knows the Father, and whose eyes look upon Jesus look upon the Father. It may be said that whoever knows God can know God through Christ, and *must* know God through Christ. And it can be said that God does always act like Christ, and Christ always acts like God, because Christ is God walking among men. It may also be said with certainty that increasing knowledge of Christ means increasing knowledge of God.

That will be a help to the heart and the mind, and I trust that God will use it to help elevate the concept of the whole evangelical church from our present Teddy Bear God to the high and lofty God that inhabits eternity.

Christ is God, acting like Himself. That is all. God is never strange. There is never any play-acting with God. God never puts on a face and never comes out and takes a character. God always acts like Himself. The most relaxed man that ever walked the streets of any city was Jesus Christ our Lord. Perfectly relaxed. He could turn calmly, look at a man, cut him to bits or draw him near and forgive his sins and heal his diseases, depending on the attitude of the person. God is always relaxed.

If God's people could only know who God is and then relax and believe Him, we would get somewhere. But as it stands now, we are either lazy or do not care anything about God, or we get hysterical. Christ never was hysterical. The only time He was ever, for even one little moment, out of control was that awful, unspeakable holy moment in the Garden of Gethsemane when He said, "Father, if thou be willing, remove this cup from me: nevertheless not my will, but thine, be done" (Luke 22:42). That was as near as He ever came in the awful agony of His death. Do not mistake hysteria for spirituality. The two are not the same.

Christ is God acting like Himself. When Jesus walked the earth, He was just God walking around acting like Himself; and when He went to the right hand of the Father, He was still God acting like Himself. When He sent the Holy Ghost down, the Holy Ghost is God acting like God. Always God acting like Himself and never out of character. He will always be the same, because that is His immutability, you see; that's what that word "immutability" means; it means He is unchanging. He will never be any different from what He is now.

People change, but God never changes. People's moods change; some people are cultivated because they read in a magazine one time about some movie actress that has moods, and so they go around moody as they can be. God bless you, honey, don't you wish you had some sense? Wouldn't it be nice if you woke up some time and rubbed your head until the circulation started? The day will come when you will be bald and have nine chins. God help you, young fellow. Think for tomorrow. Think for the future. Think about the day after tomorrow, and next year and next eternity.

Look for Holiness

The horrible travesty we have in America today is Christianity without holiness. If you say you accept Jesus, and then go raise hell, you have not accepted Jesus at all. You are a deceived man. You are no better off than if you had never heard of God. The very first qualities of Christianity are holiness, purity, right living, right thinking and right longing. But we have a Christianity today that has no holiness in it. The Son of God was a holy Son. The Father is the holy Father in heaven. And the Holy Ghost is the *Holy* Ghost. Our Bible is the Holy Bible, and the Church is called the holy Church. Heaven is a holy heaven, and the angels are holy angels. Therefore, we ought to take seriously the biblical doctrine of spirituality and holiness. Evangelical churches have fallen so far into the gutter in the day in which we live.

Jesus loved everybody. He loved them in an easy and relaxed, wonderful way. People came to Him and it made those theological Pharisees as mean as the devil. They said, "Why don't they come to us?" They did not come to them because they found no warmth there. A bird will always go to the warm side of the hill in early spring. A bobwhite used to fly around at home on the farm when the snow was almost gone. You could walk around on the dark side of the hill where the snow was and you would not find one bird. Go on over the hill and down where the sun was shining and you would find a covey of these little bobwhites waiting in the warmth. Everybody likes the warm sun when it is cold. Jesus drew people because He was God walking around acting like God in love. They did not come to the Pharisees, because the Pharisees had no love. They were a fire gone out in the stove. Nobody ever wants to stand around the stove when the fire has gone out.

Many do not know about the kind of joy we used to have on the farm in winter. We would heat a little pot-bellied stove until it was shining like a cherry. You'd come in half frozen and lean back in your chair and put your feet up on that fender around the stove. It was not so hot; it did not burn your shoes. No modern conveniences could ever beat that for sheer pleasure. Now they feed heat through little holes in the wall and do all sorts of things, and it is more convenient, I admit that, but it lacks character somehow. You just cannot fall in love with a grill.

Nobody ever comes around stoves when the fire's gone out in them. Jesus had love in His heart, and love is always warm. Love is always attractive. People come to the churches where there is warmth. They come to Christians that are warm.

The Fire of God's Love

I read a book on the Holy Spirit called *The Paraclete,* written by D. Y. Schultz. One thought that jarred me was this: Schultz said the absence of inquirers among people claiming to be filled with the Holy Ghost is a serious question whether or not they are filled with the Holy Ghost. A man says, "I'm filled with the Holy Ghost," but he never draws anybody to him. Nobody ever comes and says, "Will you help me, will you pray for me, will you tell me about the Lord, will you lift my burden, will you do something for me?" He is filled with the Spirit, but nobody comes to him.

If there is fire in the stove, you will always find a wayfarer with chilled feet and frost on his whiskers coming up near the stove.

That is why they loved Jesus Christ our Lord when He was on earth, and that's why people love Him today. They always find Him sympathetic, understanding and never sarcastic. His prophets used to, but He was always tender. He could cut the head off an old hypocrite, but He never turned on anybody that was poor and helpless and in need. He never turned on a woman taken in adultery and said, "I told you so."

He said, "Nobody else condemns you, neither do I; go on, you're forgiven" (see John 8:10-11). She went out, tears streaming down her cheeks. Couldn't He have cut her to bits and then gone on to the next town and told it as an illustration? No, that was love walking around, God's own love walking around acting like love acts.

He took those little fellows up in His arms and held them and loved them. He just acted like God, that's all. That is what God thinks of babies. That is what God thinks of those poor women. That is what God thinks of everybody that is in need.

Everyone would say of a fellow that is full of the devil that he is an odd one, and we would isolate him. He would walk around all by himself. But Jesus went and cast the devil out of him. Christ is God, acting like God, in loyalty.

Jesus—Loyal and Humble to the End

Think of the loyalty of Jesus. If ever there would have been a time when justice would have allowed Jesus to turn His back on His disciples, it was at the cross, for they all forsook Him and fled. He could have said, "Here I spent three years teaching my disciples, healing the sick, raising the dead, stilling the waters, feeding the multitude, talking of my Father's house, and I haven't one man that will stand with me. I scrape the dust off my shoes, I turn away from you." He could have done it, but you know what He did? He was loyal to that bunch of renegades and cowards who forsook Him and fled. He was loyal to the people who did not have the courage to come to His rescue. Loyal to those who would not even come out and stand and be counted. Loyal to the end, and He died loyal for those who had no loyalty for Him. Why did He have that loyalty? Was that human loyalty? Yes, but it was more than human, it was God's loyalty.

God has been loyal to the human race even though way back thousands of years ago we turned our back on Him in the person of Adam. In Adam's fall, we sinned and walked out on God. But God remembered us, kept promising down the years a Redeemer, and then a mother groaned and a baby cried, and the angels sang that God had come to earth, loyal to His renegade race. And when they took Him out to crucify Him, He was loyal still; and He's loyal at the right hand of God.

Jesus Christ will show Himself to you through faith and confession and humility. It is very hard to get people to repent because that means humility. We build up a saga about ourselves, which is why it is dangerous to be a Christian leader.

James says, "My brethren, be not many masters, knowing that we shall receive the greater condemnation" (Jas. 3:1). It is dangerous to get a saga built up about yourself. To get a reputation for being godly and then when the Holy Ghost comes and begins to lacerate your heart, you are ashamed to go to the altar, ashamed to confess, because people will think you are a hypocrite.

Humility is a beautiful thing, but not very many people have it. If I were to say, "All who want to know the Lord a little better come down to the altar," the altar would be filled and the front rows filled. If I were to say, "All that are not perfect, and would like to have the Lord bless you a little, come," we would have the altar filled and overflowing on the platform too. If I said, "Has God spoken to you, and is He calling you to confession and humility, humbleness and admission of wrong-doing?" It would be hard to get one person to come, because people do not want to humble themselves. They want to humble themselves if they could do it en masse; but they do not want to do it in the singular. This pluralizing our humility will not work. This pluralizing our confession will not work. Make it singular.

If David had got on his knees and prayed a long beautiful prayer for Israel, Psalm 51 would never have been written and David would never have gotten back to God. David said, "I did it, God, I did it. Have mercy on me, God, I did it." He singular-ized it; and if you will singularize your confession and say, "God it is I, it is I," Christ will reveal Himself to you. And as you know Christ, you will know God. Your longing to see the Father will be satisfied and your heart will know what God is like. You will have a lifetime and all eternity to build up and increase your knowledge of the infinite, incomprehensible God.

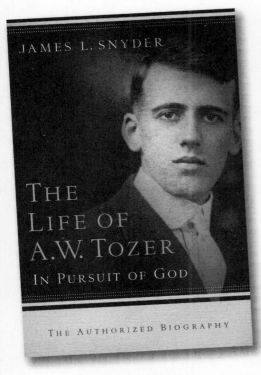

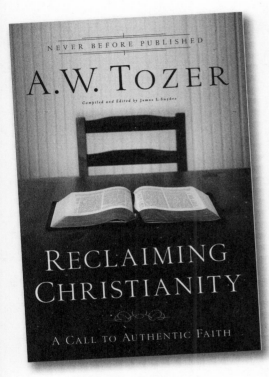